WITH

StyleCity
SAN FRANCISCO

Library

Renewals: 020 7307 2365   Email: library@fra.ac.uk

15 Gresse Street, London W1T

Contents

Street Wise

Style Traveler

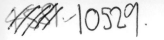

Series concept and editor: Lucas Dietrich
Jacket and book design: Grade Design Consultants
Original design and map concept: The Senate
Maps: Peter Bull

Research and texts: Deborah Bishop
Specially commissioned photography by
Anthony Webb

Although every effort has been made to ensure that
the information in this book is as up-to-date and as
accurate as possible at the time of going to press,
some details are liable to change.

First published in the United Kingdom in 2004 by
Thames & Hudson Ltd, 181A High Holborn,
London WC1V 7QX

www.thamesandhudson.com

British Library Cataloguing-in-Publication Data
A catalogue record for this book is available from the
British Library

ISBN 0-500-21010-1

Printed in China

How to Use This Guide

The book features two principal sections: **Street Wise** and **Style Traveler**.

    Street Wise, which is arranged by neighborhood, features areas that can be covered in a day (and night) on foot and includes a variety of locations – cafés, shops, restaurants, museums, performance spaces, bars – that capture local flavor or are lesser-known destinations.

    The establishments in the **Style Traveler** section represent the city's best and most characteristic locations – 'worth a detour' – and feature hotels (**sleep**), restaurants (**eat**), cafés and bars (**drink**), boutiques and shops (**shop**) and getaways (**retreat**).

    Each location is shown as a circled number on the relevant neighborhood map, which is intended to provide a rough idea of location and proximity to major sights and landmarks rather than precise position. Locations in each neighborhood are presented sequentially by map number. Each entry in the **Style Traveler** has two numbers: the top one refers to the page number of the neighborhood map on which it appears; the second number is its location.

    For example, the visitor might begin by selecting a hotel from the **Style Traveler** section. Upon arrival, **Street Wise** might lead him to the best joint for coffee before guiding him to a house-museum nearby. After lunch he might go to find a special jewelry store listed in the **shop** section. For a memorable dining experience, he might consult his neighborhood section to find the nearest restaurant crossreferenced to **eat** in **Style Traveler**.

    Street addresses are given in each entry, and complete information – including email and web addresses – is listed in the alphabetical **contact** section. Travel and contact details for the destinations in **retreat** are given at the end of **contact**.

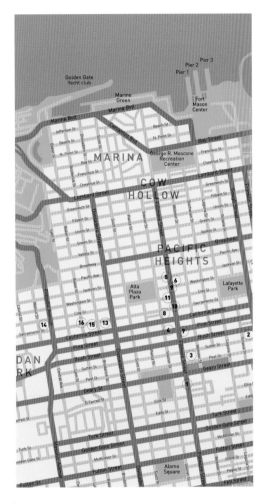

Legend

(2)   Location

           Museums, sights

           Gardens, squares

           Streets

SAN FRANCISCO

The title of poet George Sterling's 1920s ode to San Francisco — "The Cool, Grey City of Love" — could never be confused as describing any other American metropolis. Sitting at the tip of a peninsula and surrounded by water on three sides, with summer fogs that swirl across the Golden Gate Bridge and cocoon the city in a diaphanous, dove-colored shawl, San Francisco sits apart — not quite an island but certainly the quirky iconoclast and conscience of the country. No matter which way the rest of the nation may veer, San Francisco always remains reassuringly on the left. (This may be the only city whose Stock Exchange features a mural by Diego Rivera, an avowed communist.)

Esteemed by some as a Bohemian refuge, disparaged by others as a den of libertine excess since Gold Rush days, "Babylon by the Bay" may lack the gravitas of New York and share little of Los Angeles' sprawling, sun-addled glam, but it's been a fertile spawning ground for movements as earth-shaking as its notorious temblors. This is where the beat poets found their audience, where the free-speech and gay rights movements took hold, and the Summer of Love came into flower. New technologies are born here, as are "happenings" such as Burning Man, which began on a local beach. And the aftershocks of the culinary revolution fomented thirty years ago at Alice Waters's Chez Panisse are felt every time a new restaurant bases its menu on seasonal, organic ingredients.

Like any good port city, San Francisco is continually redefined by its new arrivals. In fact, the mix of cultures is embroidered into the city's history: inhabited first by Native American tribes known collectively as Costanoans (for whom arrival of the Spanish explorers and missionaries spelled eventual doom), the encampment passed to Mexico in 1821 and was annexed by the United States soon after gold was discovered in the Sierra Nevada foothills. About half the population is either foreign-born or first-generation, and a minority of inhabitants were born here. Some came to escape economic or political turmoil, others fled the stifling suburban mores of their hometowns.

People often observe that San Francisco is the most "European" of American cities, by which they tend to mean walkable and endowed with a certain innate charm. A mere seven miles by seven miles (Paul Kantner of the Jefferson Airplane once described San Francisco as "49 square miles surrounded by reality"), the city is easily traversed, from bay to breakers. And no urban planning grid could ever erase the back alleys of the old Barbary Coast that once housed opium dens and gambling joints, replace the pedestrian stairways that cut through the hills, or detract from the gift that awaits atop each steep ascent — a head-clearing, mind-blowing view of the sparkling water, bridges, Alcatraz, the Marin headlands and beyond. As for charm, much of it resides in the fact that San Francisco is comprised of explorable neighborhoods. Like small nation states, each is endowed with its own character, demographic, culture, and even microclimate — from the mural-, café-, and bar-endowed sunbelt of the Mission to the fog-washed, sanitized Marina, with its GAP-clad cadres of young professionals clutching non-fat "Frappucinos."

Interestingly, despite being a hub for cutting-edge technologies, San Francisco is weirdly protectionist about its Victorian heritage and can be almost reactionary when it comes to building vital new architecture (while blind to mediocre buildings that seem to pop up overnight). So it's not surprising that one of the most significant architectural achievements of recent years is the restoration of a 19th-century landmark. The jewel of the waterfront before falling into disuse and disrepair, the Ferry Building (page 164), is again a thriving social hub and a culinary shrine in a city that takes its food a good deal more seriously than religion.

If in most urban centers a pilgrimage is required to find untamed nature, in San Francisco it fairly surrounds you. Alistair Cooke described the "fortuitous mating of marine grandeur and terrestrial smugness" that together make this "the most individual and engaging of American cities." The meadows, tidal marshes, dunes and beaches of Crissy Field were reclaimed from a former airfield (page 94), and the Presidio offers almost 1,500 acres of pristine national parkland (page 83). Easily accessed from the Palace of the Legion of Honor (page 84) is the nine-mile Coastal Trail, where the crumbling walls of the former Adolph Sutro estate create a kind of memento mori, and the foghorns and barking of sea lions compose an atonal symphony that blends with the waves crashing against the cliffs and secluded beaches.

Indeed, despite some insurmountable problems — the unfortunate proximity of the San Andreas fault, the shocking price of real estate, and a considerable homeless population — San Francisco is a hard place to leave. When demand becomes too high, as at the height of the dot-com frenzy, the city comes perilously close to pricing itself — that is, its progressive, alternative, diverse, artsy self — right out of existence. But busts follow booms like the inevitable hangover after a night of excess, and the city mellows out to resume its role as the place of infinite possibilities. "A mad city inhabited for the most part by perfectly insane people," declared Rudyard Kipling, who nevertheless added that "San Francisco has only one drawback — 'tis hard to leave."

Street Wise

Downtown • Tenderloin • South of Market • Mission •
Potrero Hill • Civic Center • Hayes Valley • Castro •
Haight • Golden Gate Park • Financial District • Telegraph
Hill • North Beach • Chinatown • Pacific Heights • Presidio
Heights • The Presidio • Richmond • Nob Hill • Russian
Hill • Cow Hollow • Marina • Berkeley • Oakland

Downtown
Tenderloin
South of Market

The epicenter of San Francisco's downtown shopping scene is Union Square, a recently redesigned, somewhat arid granite plateau that deserved a better makeover than the one it got but is still more inviting than the enclosed, slightly sinister sea of overgrown brush designed in 1941 by Timothy Pflueger (and featured in Coppola's 1974 thriller *The Conversation*). At least people appear to be using the plaza as intended – a place to rendezvous, take an espresso, catch the sun – as well as for shortcutting diagonally past the central Corinthian column to scurry from one temple of shopping (Saks) to the other (Neiman Marcus). Within shouting distance are the monolithic megastores that make you wonder what city you're in, dozens of art galleries and designer shops (YSL, Gucci, Vuitton, Hermès), and a few independent boutiques with charm and originality – Metier (page 160), Diana Slavin (page 162) and De Vera (page 171). On Maiden Lane, the two-block pedestrian alley that houses Marc Jacobs, is Frank Lloyd Wright's only building in San Francisco, a kind of proto-Guggenheim that today is filled with ethnic artifacts (page 16).

Walking towards the Tenderloin takes you through the city's small theater district (a half-price ticket booth sits on Union Square) and the theatrical Clift hotel (page 110), a dramatic collaboration between Ian Schrager and Philippe Starck. A few more blocks and you're squarely in the Tenderloin, a magnet for hustlers and prostitutes that also serves as home to the poor. Neighborhood stalwarts like Original Joe's (page 21) share space with dive bars, some good ethnic food joints run by resident Southeast Asians and an influx of hipster watering holes with weekly DJ rosters (Olive, Julip, Hemlock). It's but a few minutes from here up to the rarefied air of Nob Hill, which remains lightyears away in every other respect.

South of Union Square is Market Street, the city's main artery, and then SoMa, which used to be "South of Market" until someone got a case of Manhattan-envy and coined the moniker, which caught on in time for the area's revitalization. A stroll down Third Street, once littered with flophouses and discarded syringes, now takes you past the Mario Botta-designed San Francisco Museum of Modern Art (page 22), the Yerba Buena Center, with its galleries, esplanade gardens, fountains and carousel (page 23); and then under a freeway overpass to South Park (page 24), most recently the frenetic headquarters of what was once "Multimedia Gulch" and now home to many old media types – architects, product designers, graphic artists and writers – as well as the cafés they require. Close by are Limn, a multi-story temple of modern design (page 27), and the city's still shiny new baseball stadium, from which home runs are cracked into the bay just beyond.

ART CRAWL

2 49 Geary Street Galleries
- Fraenkel Gallery
- 871 Fine Arts
- Catharine Clark Gallery
- Haines Gallery
- James Nicholson Gallery

Art galleries are sprinkled all around Union Square, but a good place to begin an art crawl is the building at 49 Geary, which is studded with them like raisins in a bun. A few notables include the Fraenkel, the most venerable photography gallery in the city, which has exhibited people such as Eugene Atget, Walker Evans, Edward Weston and Diane Arbus; 871 Fine Arts, a repository of 1950s and 1960s Pop Art, books and artists' ephemera, with an emphasis on California; Catharine Clark, devoted to contemporaries who push the boundaries of form and content; Haines, whose groundbreaking exhibitions have included Andy Goldsworthy, Orlan and the Young British Artists, and James Nicholson, who represents a new generation of photographers and videographers, both emerging and established. The first Thursday of each month, many downtown galleries schedule exhibition openings and stay open late, serving up art, wine and cheese to roving enthusiasts.

SMALL WONDERS

3 Murik

73 Geary Street

Murik is a common Russian name for a cat (akin to "fluffy" in English), which explains the playful, stretched-feline logo by artist Eugene Timerman adorning the awning (Danish architects Hansen and Sorensen designed the store). Folk motifs, minimalist shapes and a sophisticated palette (slate gray, wisteria, burnt orange) distinguish these Belgian, Dutch and Danish children's clothes from the pricey twee imports and mass-market brands sold at sweatshop prices. Among the designers are Jottum, Okker-Gokker, Micro Bulle and Rita Co Rita, who used to work with Dries Van Noten. "We favor and look for that classic, modern American, street-inspired look," muses Murik's owner, Elena Kirioukhina. "It just happens to be coming from northern Europe!"

AMERICAN MASTER

5 Marc Jacobs

125 Maiden Lane

In the 19th century, Maiden Lane was a red-light district and an easy place to get murdered. Fast forward a couple centuries, and the two-block pedestrian alley is a sartorial hunting ground, home to Chanel, YSL, TSE and Marc Jacobs – the wildly talented, raffish designer known for his beautifully crafted mod silhouettes and celebrity muses such as April March and Sofia Coppola. The only free-standing Marc Jacobs store outside of New York, the Stephen Jaklitsch-designed boutique houses the women's and men's collections, ladylike shoes and pocket-festooned handbags that whisper, rather than scream, the name of their creator (who also does time as artistic director for nearby Louis Vuitton). His youthful secondary line, Marc, is well represented in surrounding department stores.

PROTO-GUGGENHEIM

6 Xanadu Gallery

140 Maiden Lane

When he designed this former gift shop in 1949, Frank Lloyd Wright defied store-layout logic with the cavelike, arched-brick entryway and an interior ramp that spirals upward, echoing the layout of its larger cousin, New York's Guggenheim Museum. Crowned with a bulbous acrylic skylight, the magnificent circular space with porthole cutouts lost its luster under indifferent owners until local architect Aaron Green (who had completed the Wright-designed Marin County Civic Center after Wright's death) was hired to oversee its renovation. Armed with original prints and photos, Green restored the curved walnut cases and brass and acrylic display stands that were languishing in the basement and found the original manufacturer to replace the skylight. Walls were painted the pale yellow that Wright specified (but that had never been used). Today, the store looks as if it might have been custom-designed for its current collection of Asian, African and Oceanic sculpture, artifacts and jewelry – from Chinese ceramics to carved Ethiopian stools and rare Baltic amber.

In the city where blue jeans were born, two temples of denim draw their own devoted acolytes. Levi's traces its lineage to the Gold Rush, when an immigrant named Levi Strauss began selling miners durable blue workpants with riveted stress points, little imagining that his descendants would one day diversify the hardworking trousers into so many leisure-appropriate permutations. A block away, Italy's Diesel fills five floors with its juiced-up designs, fabrics and finishes, including the futuristic StyleLab line and tiny, scaled-down togs for future club kids – from tops embellished with embroidery and hip-hop graphics to cozy hats that would not look amiss on Mongolian shepherds.

Although the brand that was sparked by a single tote bag is evolving into a chain of sorts, this outpost has its charms. Geometric-print nylon bags, leather goods in Lily Pulitzer colors and post-preppy shoes are arrayed amongst Risom armchairs, an Arne Vodder daybed and a Calderesque light fixture by David Weeks that draws architects in for a closer look. There are also vintage books on offer (in Paul Smith tradition), from collectible Cecil Beatons to Sam Haskins' sixties-era photographic classic *Five Girls*, and cool old paintings (regrettably not for sale).

Café Claude sits on a tiny, mews-like alley that hasn't changed much since its cameo in the flowershop scene in *Vertigo*. A few tables edge onto the street, or you can dine at red booths on cuisine a bit more modern than the furnishings – famously rescued from Le Barbizan, a café in Paris about to be demolished. Lunch is bustling and businesslike, while dinner turns more romantic and the food more adventurous, with live jazz and special happenings (such as a Serge Gainsbourg tribute).

Belden Place was a dusty financial district back alley before Eric Klein and Olivier Azancot colonized it with Café Bastille, then convinced the city to close the street to traffic in the higher interest of consuming hachis parmentier and crème caramel *en plein air*. Next they partnered with Jocelyn Bulow to open Plouf ("splash"), a seafood restaurant known for mussels prepared myriad ways and buff waiters in striped sailor shirts, who emerge through a huge metal door that's riveted like a ship (designed by Larissa and Jeff Sand of South Park Fabricators). Also designed by the South Park team was B44, where chef Daniel Olivella requested a cool, urban backdrop for his modern Catalan cuisine ("no toros, tapas, bull fighters or flamencos!"). Pendant lights emit a saffron glow, and in the restrooms, images of traditional festivities from Olivella's hometown of Vilafranca del Peneddes flicker on inset video monitors. And at DJ bar Voda, the draw is infused vodkas in flavors like apricot, honey and licorice. Today the alley is an animated sea of tables, umbrellas and diners who descend at the first rumor of sunshine.

A fine place to slip in for a cocktail and nurse fantasies of living in a Graham Greene novel, Le Colonial transformed Trader Vic's (a longtime tiki-themed clubhouse for the social set) into 1920s French colonial-era Vietnam with palm fronds, lazy overhead fans, an upstairs lounge with rattan couches and vintage lamps, and a semi-sheltered verandah. A pot of tea or signature cocktail – guava, citrus vodka and splash of soda – eases the transition from day to night, and much of the fresh French–Vietnamese cuisine (the original fusion?) can be taken at the bar.

Like a lot of neighborhood bars, the Owl Tree has low lighting, stiff drinks and a jukebox filled with pre-techno crooners. Unlike any other drinking establishment we know, it's a shrine to the obsession of its somewhat taciturn owner, Bobby Cobby, who has been collecting owl-themed items in every iteration since he was too young to sip anything but milk. The wide-eyed nocturnal birds cover every inch of the bar – even the menus are owl-shaped – and the stock is regularly supplemented by the bar's regulars, or "night owls," as Cobby (affectionately) calls them.

An emporium of pulp fiction from the 1940s onward, Kayo specializes in vintage paperbacks with alluring cover art and provides "a glimpse into the lurid past of dimestore novels, sleazy 1960s exploitation and 1970s pop culture."

With categories such as Hard-boiled Mystery, Hippies and Drugs, Sleaze and Erotica and Bizarre Non-Fiction, Kayo stakes out different ground than your typical antiquarian bookshop (much of its inventory is five dollars and under) and offers such promising titles as "Psycho Circus," "Love me Sailor" and "Brutal Ecstasy," although there are also collectible classics by authors such as Ed Wood, John Steinbeck and Dashiell Hammett.

EVOLVED OPULENCE

22 Fleur de Lys

136

ORAL TRADITIONS

23 Edinburgh Castle

950 Geary Street

Bartender, writer and impresario Alan Black runs the show at this pub-cum-performance place, which we'll let him describe: "Fortified against the wave of urban madness that swarms the streets of the Tenderloin district, the Castle is an oasis of culture, fueled by strong drink and food wrapped in newspaper." (The list of single-malt scotches is reassuringly long and the nearby Old Chelsea delivers piping hot fish and chips.) Big and drafty, kitted out with weird chandeliers, heraldic symbols, booths and dim corners, the bar stages plays – including the American premiere of *Trainspotting* (Irvine Welsh is a frequent guest), sponsors readings (J. T. Leroy, Patrick McCabe and Black – himself a wildly talented scribbler), hosts local bands, and produces events such as Orwell Night and Litquake. And the crowd? Back to Alan: "Young hipsters, middle-aged hippies, nutters and mutterers from all 'round the globe."

OLD HAUNT

24 Original Joe's

144 Taylor Street

A veil of history and grease hangs over Original Joe's, a beacon in these now mean streets, which opened in 1937 (the tuxedoed waiters look as if they've been there since the start). Even with burgers, chops, fish and steaks the size of Rhode Island, Joe's isn't a total foodie anachronism: they've always used mesquite in the grill, the bread is from the Italian–French Bakery in North Beach, and the bacon is smoked over apple wood. An ideal place to slip onto a barstool or into a booth (from mid-morning till midnight), sink into a real Martini, and observe the mix of SF society – from claques of attorneys to post-show hipsters to a homeless man enjoying a bowl of soup on the house.

25 SFMOMA
151 3rd Street

Swiss Architect Mario Botta's 1995 brick-faced building is topped with a circular skylight that illuminates its four floors of galleries and vertigo-inducing top-story catwalk. The decent, if somewhat scattered, permanent collection includes everyone from Mondrian to Rothko to Koons, while long lines are generated by traveling shows – such as retrospectives of Eva Hesse, Gerhard Richter and Marc Chagall. The museum is especially strong in the photography and digital arts department, with a respected permanent collection and special exhibitions ranging from Charles Dodgson's Victorian prints of Alice Liddell to works by Andreas Gursky and Diane Arbus. Admission is half-price on Thursday evenings, which tends to spawn a considerable social scene amongst the young professional set.

26 Yank Sing
One Rincon Center, 101 Spear Street

Chef Henry Chan's downtown dim sum houses (founded by his father in 1958) effectively channel a modern, bustling Hong Kong teahouse ambience while providing an appreciative audience for his "creative collection" – which greatly expands upon the traditional hors d'oeuvre-sized dumplings. (Sometimes he is moved to dispense with the wrapping entirely, as when serving tender slices of Peking duck or sea bass with basil.) But even the 70 or so more familiar offerings – from barbecued pork buns to translucent dumplings plump with shrimp or shiitake mushrooms – that go whizzing by on carts are distinguished by their freshness and execution. Wander to the adjacent Art Déco Rincon Annex Post Office Building for a look at Russian-born artist Anton Refregier's 1941 murals, which caused a stir for their portrayal of some less-than-illustrious events in the region's history.

CULTURE CLUB
27 Yerba Buena Center for the Arts
701 Mission Street

Facing off across Third Street like SFMOMA's hipper, more alternative cousin (the one with the pierced brow), Yerba Buena is a multimedia mecca. The complex of theaters and galleries plays host to films (from underground to world premieres), art exhibits (subjects have included boxing, surfing, archival crime photographs and a Pierre et Gilles retrospective); lectures on design and technology, and performing arts (from hip-hop to Ballet Preljocaj). There's even a carousel, circa 1906, located at the entrance to Zeum, the children's art and technology center. And the five acres of gardens and fountains create a bucolic setting for a personal installation: you and your lunch.

JAPANESE SPLURGE
28 Kyo-Ya
136

COMIC GENIUS
29 Cartoon Art Museum
665 Mission Street

San Francisco has been a hotbed of comic art since the 1960s, when cartoonists such as Robert Crumb helped launch the underground comix movement from the Haight Ashbury. This museum (the only one of its type in the country) is devoted to the preservation of an art form that is often thought of as disposable. Housing a bookstore, research library and collection of 6,000 original pieces, it also mounts several exhibitions a year – from shows on Alternative Comic Art to hep comic cats from Felix to Fritz.

HIGH TEA AND TONICS
30 Garden Court and Pied Piper Bar
150

31 111 Minna Gallery

154

32 Varnish
77 Natoma Street

Sculptors Kerri Stephens and Jennifer Rogers spent some fifteen-odd years toiling in other people's foundries when, says Stephens, "We decided to take a look at the art world from the other side!" They like the view from this big and airy gallery down a narrow South of Market alleyway not far from the bus terminal. For another incentive to linger, they also installed a DJ and wine bar. The interesting list includes many quirky California varietals (plus a few fruity sake cocktails) and Tuesday night is flight night. Although the approach sounds similar to neighboring art bar/club 111 Minna, the vibe at Varnish is mellower – more about the art and less about the music.

33 430 Clementina
- Hosfelt Gallery
- Braunstein/Quay Gallery

These galleries sharing a common façade belong to the respected downtown art world, yet stand slightly apart – both in spirit and geography. Installed in a converted warehouse transformed by San Francisco architect Anne Fougeron on a South of Market alley, they are off the beaten path and best known for showing provocative work (as well as for their lively opening parties). Hosfelt focuses somewhat on pattern painting and drawing, video and electronic media and site-specific installations. Braunstein/Quay, which moved from digs downtown, helped advance the modern ceramics movement and also features sculpture and mixed media.

34 Sixth Street District
- Anú, 43 Sixth Street
- Arrow Bar, 10 Sixth Street
- Lit, 101 Sixth Street
- Six, 60 Sixth Street
- Luggage Store, 1007 Market Street
- Tu Lan, 8 Sixth Street

It's a classic urban cycle: people discover an "edgy" part of town, colonize it, then flock there in droves, often to the bemusement of the area's permanent denizens. Lined with liquor stores and tenement hotels, this mini skid row has become a magnet for DJ bars (to which people tend to pull-up while watching their backs). Anú is a lovely, low-key lounge with jewel-toned lamps and a selection of infused vodkas, a much calmer counterpoint to throbbing Arrow Bar across the street. Lit's urban burlesque lounge ambiance melds DJs and assorted live acts with the original 1860s bar décor. And Six, which spawned the whole movement, has a main floor devoted to acid house and an upstairs lounge blasting "booty bass." Some come to drink after an opening at the Luggage Store, an alternative non-profit gallery around the corner. Others move on to dine at Tu Lan, a bare-bones dive that has long served some of the city's freshest Vietnamese food, famously praised by chef Julia Child.

35 South Park
Bounded by 2nd & 3rd Streets, Bryant, & Brannan

This oval-shaped greensward a few blocks from Jack London's birthplace was designed during the Gold Rush boom to resemble a classic London terrace. But its opening collided with an economic bust, and by the time the city acquired the park in 1897, many of its gracious villas had been reborn as rooming houses. Charmed by this urban Arcadia, artists and designers started migrating in the 1980s and were rewarded with low rents, cafés and quirky shops. The area started to tread a comfortable middle ground between boho and bourgeois when the dot-commies descended and ordained South Park as multimedia gulch's ground zero, causing rents to spiral and original tenants to flee. Now that reality has returned, this oasis of green is again a quiet hideout, unseen even by many who pass on their way to the ballpark.

36 South Park Café
108 South Park

This café with buttery yellow walls and painted wooden banquettes gamely opened its doors more than fifteen years ago. Today, owner/chef Ward Little continues to serve bistro fare in a congenial setting with a few sidewalk tables for precious warm nights. Niçoise pizza with brandade and roasted tomatoes, a braised beef "en daube" with olives and a hint of orange, and ahi tuna tartare with a mound of crisp frites always satisfy, and the three-course fixed-price dinner remains one of the better values around.

430 Clementina

Braunstein/Quay Gallery
Hosfelt Gallery

Tuesday – Saturday 11:00 – 5:30

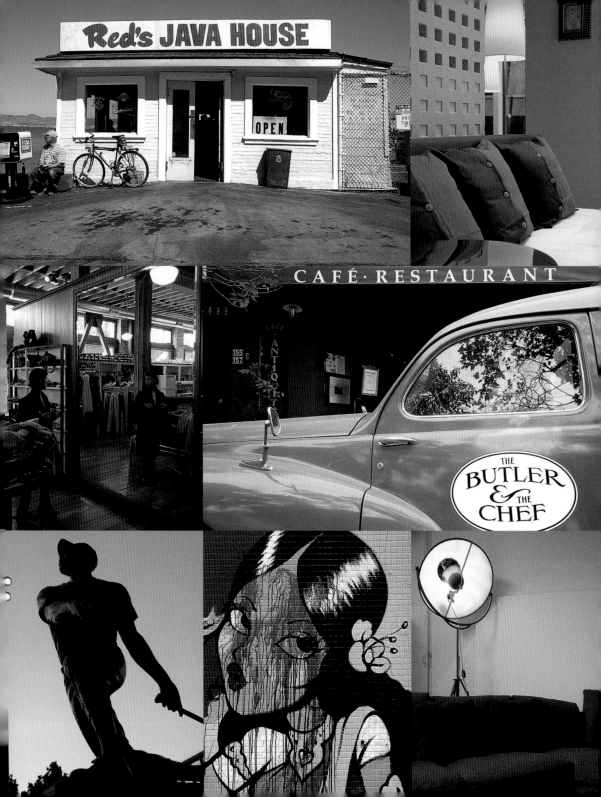

DISCOUNT DIVAS
37 Jeremys
2 South Park

Whether it's an op-art Marni skirt that costs a month's mortgage, a pre-frayed Comme des Garçons tartan jacket or those Miu Miu or Manolo mules, there's a good chance that these, or something equally enthralling, will migrate to a rack at Jeremy's by season's end – brand new but with an emaciated price. Women and men make pilgrimages to this airy, wood-paneled store both for the big names and for the equally fetching pieces without pedigrees. Part of the thrill is never knowing what you'll find and of course being reunited with those Marc jeans at a third their former price.

PARK VIEWS
38 The Butler & the Chef
155A South Park
Caffe Centro
102 South Park

A grey 1952 Peugeot truck sits parked in front of The Butler & the Chef, which serves morning crème and croissants, lunch crepes and croques and afternoon Pernod. Pierre Chatel's amiable and bustling café is like a slice of Paris – literally. The tables, the bowls, the bistro chairs on which you're parked are all for sale, supplied by the Butler & the Chef store (1011 25th Street, at Third), which is crammed with everything from old zinc bars to refectory tables, butcher blocks and Calvados glasses, and makes one wonder if there can possibly be anything left in the old country. Across the green Caffe Centro has attracted lines during boom and lean times with its fresh and often organic fare, metal tables positioned to catch the sun and friendly staff who play excellent tunes throughout the day.

MODERN OBJECTS
39 Limn
290 Townsend Street

"I guess you could find much of what we show elsewhere, but it would take traipsing to fifteen different places to do so," says Dan Friedlander of Limn, his multi-story cathedral to 20th-century furniture, lighting and accessories. Friedlander calls his store a "love affair with objects and furniture." This is the place that introduced Memphis (and Sottsass) to America, has championed the likes of Noguchi, Rietveld, Thonet and others, and where you go to see that Droog sink from the Salone di Mobile in person. Limn's art gallery also mounts rotating shows –

such as a recent multimedia look at urban architecture and its relationship to the environment.

DESIGN SHRINE
40 Ligne Roset
162 King Street

Facing the baseball stadium across the street in strange counterpoint is one of many Ligne Roset showrooms in the world – but the only one owned by Dan Friedlander, founder of nearby Limn. To interpret the pale palette that traditionally serves as backdrop to the contemporary furnishings, Friedlander engaged designer Tarik Currimbhoy to place marble (from the same Indian quarries used for the Taj Mahal) that had been variously honed, beaten, polished and textured to look like pebbles, while moveable walls allow the space to ebb and flow.

FIELD OF DREAMS
41 SBC (formerly Pacbell) Park
King Street

In San Francisco the "National Pastime" is played in a new stadium imbued with enough old-fashioned feeling to inspire nostalgia even in those who don't follow the sport, as does the statue of Giants great Willie Mays in action. Perched at the water's edge, the ballpark (whose moniker reflects the sad trend of granting naming rights to corporate bidders) also reflects the city's egalitarian yearnings. There's an observation area where one can watch three innings of any game free, the Giants' owner reportedly inspired by a Norman Rockwell painting of a child peering longingly through the knothole of a fence.

ON THE WATERFRONT
42 Red's Java House
The Embarcadero, Pier 30

When strolling along the Embarcadero, with its myriad opportunities for espresso, microbrewed beer, sushi and foie gras, it's a tonic to stumble across a bona fide dive that recalls an era when this was a working waterfront. Red's has held its ground on Pier 30 (at Bryant Street) since 1923, a salt-air cured, pine-paneled shack that dispenses beer, burgers, fries and your basic dog (the menu is nailed to the wall) and a million-dollar view, with the background music provided by the gulls.

43 SF Camerawork
1246 Folsom Street

This thirty-year-old non-profit gallery expresses its devotion to the photographic medium through exhibitions, a journal, bookstore and lectures (from Mary Ellen Mark to William Wegman). The shows are often provocative and might take the form of video, film or related technologies. A recent exhibit from the Mütter Museum of Philadelphia (one of the last medical museums surviving from the 19th century) mixed archival images with new work by contemporary photographers of medical curiosities ranging from human horns to murderers' brains.

GO-GO FISH
44 Sushi Groove South
1516 Folsom Street

Equal parts sushi and groove – and too cool to have a sign – this candlelit room along the nightlife stretch of Folsom Street was conceived by party promoters Martel Toler and Nabiel Musleh after their first Sushi Groove opened on Russian Hill. They expanded the menu (the original restaurant has no kitchen) and added a DJ. While the usual nigiri offerings are available, most come for the creative rolls, such as Techno Maki (an assortment of glistening fresh fish rolled inside out) and specials such as tuna caliente, a kind of tuna tartare spiked with jalapeno and green onions – and of course, the cocktails and unfiltered sakes served in chilled Martini glasses.

SHAKE IT
45 The Stud
399 9th Street

Hot today and gone tomorrow, San Francisco dance clubs come and go with the frequency of California's governors and are best discovered by word of mouth. Except for some, like The Stud, which arrived in 1966 and isn't going anywhere. It's not the trendiest or the flashiest club in town. Just a good place to get down, and one of the few that doesn't subscribe to the "separate-but-equal" ethos that seems to segregate gays and straights when it's time to party. Although there's a different theme every night of the week, Saturday's "Sugar" spins house until 4am, and "TrannyShack" Tuesday is a legend in its own time.

DÉLICES DE CALIFORNIE
46 Chez Spencer

130

EAST GERMAN CHIC
47 Walzwerk
381 South Van Ness Avenue

"For many years the food we've grown up with was hidden behind a wall. Now anyone in San Francisco is allowed a taste. We've even learned to use vegetables!" Willkommen to Walzwerk, a cozy little slice of 1960s East Germany with social realist décor and sweetly mismatched crockery, where your hosts, Christiane Schmidt and Isabell Mysyk, soothe the masses with hearty red beet soup, matjes herring salad in sour cream with apples and onions, a land mass of schnitzel on an islet of mashed potatoes, and their special Thüringer bratwurst with sauerkraut – proletarian bliss washed down with one of the many German beers on tap and in bottles.

CULINARY MISSION
48 Woodward's Garden
1700 Mission Street

The most elaborate of the edifying amusement gardens so popular in 19th-century San Francisco, Woodward's took up two city blocks and contained a zoo, museums and an aquarium. A century and a half later, this tiny restaurant (with archival photos) sits on the same spot as the former garden's entrance, an oft-deserted corner where SoMa abuts the Mission. Despite (or perhaps because of) its dubious locale, Woodward's Garden is consistently voted "most romantic" by locals. Perhaps it's the way the lace curtains hanging in the window conspire with the wind-blown newspapers on the sidewalk to confer a kind of Edward Hopper charm. Certainly, the food is also a draw. Dana Tommasino (who cooked at Greens) and partner Margie Conard fairly cram their small menu with organic ingredients in fascinating combinations (a garden salad of grilled figs, chevre, sweet walnuts and arugula; a grilled pork chop served with plum-shallot sauce, garlic-mashed potatoes and a triad of French, Romano and wax beans). Now open as a café, it has a daytime menu offering organic coffee, morning pastries, panini and weekend brunch.

Mission
Potrero Hill

The city's oldest neighborhood, the Mission, was settled by the Spanish in the 1770s (Mission Dolores, page 38, is the city's oldest standing structure), who were followed by Irish, Germans and Italians before Mexican and Central American émigrés transformed the area into a true Latino quarter with Spanish-language movie theaters, mercados, dance clubs and taquerias. They in turn were joined by artists, students and other arrivistes attracted by the warm weather, low rents and atmosphere of Bohemian bonhomie fueled by late-night bars and cafés (and willing to put up with less salubrious elements such as drug dealers, prostitutes and gang-related mayhem).

Some feared the Mission would lose its groove when the young tech wizards started moving in with fistfuls of dollars and pushing out the neighborhood's then-indigenous peoples — longtime residents and non-profit and arts organizations. Since the dot-com demise, the neighborhood is calmer, though still a magnet for those seeking to soak up some of that Mission cool. Today, the partially gentrified district is a lively mix of quirky shops and vintage clothing stores, especially along Valencia Street, dive and DJ bars, and some of the city's finest restaurants and cafés (Delfina, page 132, Tartine, page 147). Every November 2, a somber but spirited procession winds through the streets to mark Dia de los Muertos, candles lighting up the dark and noisemakers rattling into the crisp night air laced with the smell of burning sage. Altars to the dearly departed are set up en route, especially along Balmy Alley, which is also home to many of the 200 murals splashed across walls and garages in the district.

Also in the Mission is one park where good weather and vegetation converge. Bounded by Dolores, Church, 18th and 20th Streets, the huge, hilly blanket of greenery, palm trees, tennis courts and soccer fields called Dolores Park was first inhabited by the Ohlone Indians, followed by Spanish ranchers and Gold Rush merchants, and for a brief spell served as a Jewish cemetery. A year after its purchase by the city, the area became a refugee camp for families made homeless by the 1906 earthquake. Above the park some especially steep streets offer glimpses of the kind of decorative Victorian houses that end up on postcards, especially along Liberty Street.

From the Mission it's an easy stroll eastward to Potrero Hill, currently morphing from a pleasant and sunny residential neighborhood into a serious dining destination along 18th Street, most notably with Chez Papa (page 41) and Baraka (page 141). And when you cross Third Street and see water, you've hit China Basin, whose gritty industrial demeanor may soon be altered by development, but where a few dive bars still serve up bloody Marys dockside.

1   Scuderia West

69 Duboce Avenue

Zeitgeist

199 Valencia Street

It's not only the friendliest but the best-stocked bike shop in town – and likely the only one with a monolithic counter sculpted from a ship's hull. In addition to the bikes (KTM, Aprilia) and scooters there's masses of accessories, fan gear, messenger bags by local faves Timbuk2, and a full range of leathers for women and children by Dainesi and Vanson. Scuderia also makes a special effort to squeeze travelers' bikes in for a service (it does help to have a good story). Across the street, archetypal biker bar Zeitgeist is down and dirty on the inside and has an Arcadian beer garden out back covered with picnic tables, where bike messengers and others blessed with flexible schedules go to enjoy their burgers and pint-sized bloody Marys *en plein air*.

MOLTEN MAGIC

2   Pauline's Pizza Pie

260 Valencia Street

Many of the imaginative ingredients topping the thin-crusted pizzas and tossed into the organic salads taste so fresh because they were just plucked from the back garden (lemon thyme, nasturtium flowers, frisée lettuce). The servers can also be pretty fresh on any given night, but it doesn't matter once your fragrant pesto or meyer lemon purée, feta and pancetta pizza hit the table. Butcher paper on top of the linen tablecloths and the glass of colored crayons gives one something to do during the wait.

UNDERGROUND ART

3   Jack Hanley Gallery

389 & 395 Valencia Street

A star in the constellation of Mission district galleries operating outside the established downtown art solar system (others include nearby Pond and 66 Balmy), Jack Hanley's fierce interest in works on paper and nose for the quirky have made this an especially bright – and hip – gathering place for the perusal of outsider art and more. His openings are not only great parties (though you're more likely to find a keg than a case of Cabernet) but have helped restore a sense of freshness and discovery to the whole endeavor.

MIXED MEDIA

4   Intersection for the Arts

446 Valencia Street

Knowing that this unassuming storefront houses the city's "oldest alternative art space" makes it sound a good deal less interesting than it is. Some of the most vital drama in the city takes place in its tiny theater, including works by playwright-in-residence Denis Johnson (award-winning author of *Jesus' Son*) and cofounded by actor and writer Sean San Jose. Intersection's gallery supports new and established artists, such as British activist Conrad Atkinson. And jam sessions by jazz musicians and performances by resident composer Marcus Shelby and his 16-piece orchestra attract yet another following.

JUKE JOINT

5   Dalva

3121 16th Street

Somewhere between a dive and a lounge, Dalva (named for a book by Jim Harrison) is the progenitor of the hipster Mission district bar, yet has avoided the fate of most of its imitators: it's still cool. Situated next to the Roxie theater (classic revivals and indie releases), Dalva is perfect for a pre-film cocktail or house sangria, with entertainment by Orpheus, a legendary jukebox filled with the likes of Arab Strap, DJ Krush, Zap Mama, 1,000 Clowns and Air. Or come after ten to find blue votives flickering and a DJ spinning everything from drum 'n' bass to Afro–Cuban as you drift from the front bar to the labyrinth of back rooms.

SEE AND BE SCENE

6   Luna Park

137

21ST-CENTURY BURGER

7   Burger Joint

807 Valencia Street

The décor is Jetsons's retro-future, but there's nothing passé about the burgers, made from locally raised and naturally fed Niman Ranch beef (suppliers to most of the city's chi-chi restaurants). The chicken breast is similarly free-range and the hotdogs hormone-free, and there are veggie burgers for those who shun the eating of critters. Add a malt thick enough to use as spackling and a plate of fries and settle into a ruby booth, beneath one of local artist Scott Hamilton's colorful stencil paintings.

CURIOUSER AND CURIOUSER

8 Paxton Gate

HIP LIT 101

9 826 Valencia

826 Valencia Street

At San Francisco's only independent pirate supply store, embellished by a newly minted mural on the façade by artist/writer Chris Ware, the wooden floor is not unlike a ship's deck and the listing cabinets offer a goodly supply of flags, eye patches, glass eyes, and peg legs (there's also a capacious vat of lard and a pufferfish named Karl). As it happens, 826 Valencia is also an outpost of the McSweeney's publishing enterprise, stocking all of the company's books and journals, from the *McSweeney's Quarterly* to *The Believer*. But in the back is the place's raison d'etre: a writing lab and drop-in tutoring center for students from age eight to eighteen that offers free workshops in everything from "Short Story to Computer Programming" and "Ironic Fairy Tales" to "Making Poems" and "Record Your Own Darn Songs." It's all supported, in part, by sales of lard, so come in and have a look, matey.

NEIGHBORHOOD TAPAS

10 Timo's

842 Valencia Street

Carlos "Timo" Corredor was making his exuberant tapas long before small plates became a San Francisco fetish. His voluminous menu of more than sixty variations includes offerings for the adventurous – frog legs, lamb kidneys – alongside signature dishes like potato decadence (Yukon golds, wild and tame mushrooms, garlic and marjoram), nuggets of grilled fish with choice of romesco, aioli and roasted habanero, and a Catalan-style rabbit redolent of cinnamon and bitter chocolate. The series of brightly colored rooms in this former bar conspires with the list of Spanish and Californian varietals, sangria and cocktails to evoke something like a nightly party.

MOD SQUAD

11 Den

849 Valencia Street

X21 Modern

890 Valencia Street

Den and X21 face off across the street like the odd couple of hipster furniture stores. You could feel comfortable moving into Den, where Louisiana native Raymond Long

mixes mid-century masters with contemporary pieces by Bay Area designers and artists (one wall is reconceived every other week by painter John Baden) along with Danish ceramics and African artifacts. The soft-spoken Long is extending the Den brand into other areas, from affordable private-label furniture to a compilation of local musicians. At X21, the thrill is in roaming the cavernous space filled with "modern design classics, folk-funk oddities and spent urban debris," as proprietor Quinn Luke puts it, and blowing the dust off that vintage steel Bertoia child's chair, Arne Jacobsen dining set or aluminum gargoyle table before the dealers beat you to it.

DESIGN MISSION

12 hrm

924 Valencia Street

Polished and modern, hrm is more NoLIta than Mission District and it's not surprising to learn that the designers also wholesale to boutiques in New York and beyond. Men come for Bob Scales's Egyptian cotton shirts, zip-front jackets and straight-leg trousers that update 1960s suit pants, and to check out limited-edition "Orange Label" pieces, such as a jacket made from oiled wool army blankets and the intricately embroidered silk organza shirts. For her women's line ("House of Hengst"), Susan Hengst plays with patterns and uses the undersides of fabrics to beautiful effect. Her cashmere blend Church Coat pairs raw edges with a sleek silhouette and the hooded, plush Bunny Coat is sculpted to hug the body.

MAGICAL SLIPPERS

13 Laku

1069 Valencia Street

Yaeko Yamashita sits at her sewing machine in the back of this tiny, jewel box of a shop-cum-atelier (named for her son) with worn wood floors and vintage mannequins, where she makes the hand-stitched baby shoes and precious slippers that look as if they stepped out of some exotic fairy tale. Wrought from velvet, shantung silk, wool and the softest kid leather, each is a confection, topped with rosettes, dots, buttons and curlicues and available in all sizes, from tiny to full-grown. She also creates enchanting Lilliputian hats and clothing as well as jewelry, handbags and hair adornments for big girls.

BOÎTE NOIRE

14 Lone Palm

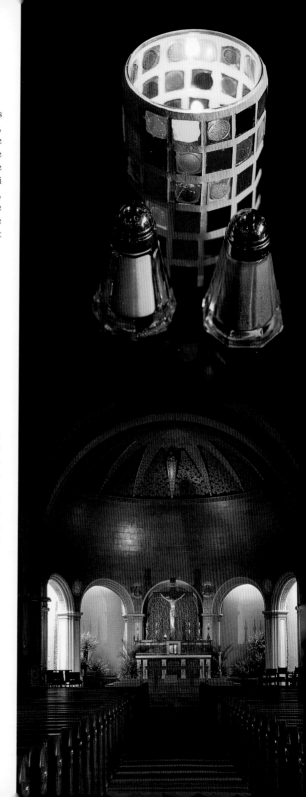

NEW WORLD PERUVIAN
15 Limón
3316 17th Street

When Martin Castillo (a veteran of culinary stalwarts Stars, Rubicon and Aqua) decided to cook from his heart, he enlisted his mother and three brothers to help create the carta of contemporary twists on authentic Peruvian cuisine – empanadas filled with beef, egg and raisins; a ceviche platter piled with lime-marinated halibut, shrimp, calimari and octopus with a side of steamed yams, and lomo saltado, tender slices of beef sauteed with onions and tomatoes. The tiny industrial storefront with lime exterior and tangerine walls feels air-lifted from an Almodovar film and the fruit ice cream is flown in from Peru.

SWEET AND SAVORY
16 Tartine Bakery

ITALIAN SOUL FOOD
17 Delfina

GASTRONOMIC DELIGHTS
18 Bi-Rite Market
3639 18th Street

Bi-Rite opened its doors in 1940 and was restored to its former luster by the brothers Mogannam, sons of the original owner. Whether you want a picnic for Dolores Park or crave a night in, Bi-Rite has the goods without gourmet-shop pretensions or miles of aisles: fresh organic produce, dozens of interesting cheeses and wines. But the deli case sings a particularly seductive siren song – with house-cured salmon, smoked trout, roasted chicken, fresh-made Italian sausages, an array of creative organic salads and made-to-order sandwiches. Artisanal ice creams, chocolates and house-baked cookies also abound.

COLONIAL SURVIVOR
19 Mission Dolores
3321 16th Street

Long before Hitchcock shot *Vertigo*'s graveyard scene in its charming little cemetery, Mission Dolores was established by Father Junipero Serra as the sixth of his twenty-one missions. Built in 1791 (and restored in 1916 by Willis Polk), the original chapel has thick adobe walls, a gilded Baroque altar brought by mule from Mexico, and ceiling painted with vegetable dyes by local Native Americans –

it's the oldest standing structure in the city. Many notable San Franciscans are buried in the cemetery, where an inscribed pedestal alludes to the devastation wrought by colonial ambitions – some 5,000 Native Americans were wiped out by measles and buried in a mass grave. Today, the church and gardens offer a cool retreat from city strife.

SENEGALISE BEATS AND BREWS
20 Bissap Baobab

JAZZ: FROM CLASSIC TO ACID
21 Bruno's
2389 Mission Street

In this once hep-cat town of nightspots and speakeasies, only a handful of live jazz joints remain. Bruno's is a forties-era *Goodfellas* restaurant with a club in the back. A Mondrian-inspired glass partition leads to the swanky bar area, which channels Rat Pack style through multicolored cylindrical lighting, leather booths and a 500-gallon fish tank burbling behind the bar. Touring acts and local luminaries entertain in the often packed back room .

COOL WATERING HOLE
22 Laszlo

DINNER AND A FLICK
23 Foreign Cinema

135

FRESH MEXICAN
24 La Taqueria

143

SALSA SUNDAYS
25 El Rio
3158 Mission Street

This sprawling club, loosely decorated with holiday lights, veers from Arabian Nights on Thursdays to world music on Fridays. But the draw is Sunday afternoons, when a huge swathe of San Francisco society – straight, gay, young ravers, less-young professionals, art students and tech-heads – gather on the outdoor garden patio for margaritas and the weekly democratizing salsa fest that gets underway at four and wraps at the civilized hour of eight o'clock.

COUNTER CULTURE
26 Blue Plate

GRUB AND DUB
27 Emmy's Spaghetti Shack
18 Virginia Avenue

Emmy's is everything you want a dive to be – small, dark, cheap – in addition to which it has more-than-decent food. A huge bowl of spaghetti with meatballs will set you back a mere $8.50, although there are all kinds of edibles, from asparagus and goat-cheese tart to organic greens and grilled sweet potatoes. DJs spin on the weekends and Sarah, the Barbadian chef, is sometimes inspired to pull out her collection of rare instrumental reggae and Grace Jones dub. A string of vintage aprons constitutes the décor, and the bar dispenses cocktails, wine, ale and 40-ouncers of domestic brew.

FOLK AND FINE ART
28 Galeria de la Raza and Studio 24
2857 24th Street

Local artists active in el Movimiento (the Chicano civil rights movement) founded this non-profit gallery thirty years ago as a venue for Latin-American artists exploring themes relevant to their community through everything from performance art to cyber-installations. In a recent exhibition, Armando Rascon created a postmodern shrine to evoke the world as viewed through the eyes of a border crosser making a pilgrimage to the chapel. The gallery is supported in part by Studio 24, a gift shop stocked with hip "Latinobilia," and traditional folk art for Dia de los Muertos.

CRAFTED COMFORT FOOD
29 Universal Café

DIAMOND IN THE ROUGH
30 Slow Club
2501 Mariposa Street

When the dot-com era crashed, eateries in this Mission–Potrero hood started fading away like the Cheshire Cat's smile. But this concrete-and-glass jewelbox still rests on a corner, candles flickering and hip moodiness undisturbed. The industrial demeanor is a reflection of the surroundings rather than fashion (there's a bus storage facility across the street), and chef Sante Salvoni keeps lunch and dinner prices easy while adding Mediterranean

riffs at the open kitchen: prosciutto and grilled peach with marinated goat cheese, grilled merguez sausage, pan-roasted halibut on French lentils and one of the city's best burgers. Weekend brunch brings sweet risotto with raisins, toasted walnuts and maple syrup.

MOORISH TAPAS
31 Baraka

PROVENCE IN POTRERO
32 Chez Papa Bistrot
1404 18th Street

Even in this bistro-laden city, tiny, packed Chez Papa and its urbane take on Provence have people crossing town for a place at one of the zinc tables. In true San Francisco style, chef Ola Fendert (who also oversees nearby Baraka) and the team from downtown Plouf offer a plethora of small plates – mushroom ravioli with fried sage, potato salad with artichokes and asparagus, prawns laced with Pastis – and a handful of larger ones, such as roasted chicken with olives and lemon. A block away, Chez Maman serves crepes and a succinct menu of Provençal standards in a cozy, converted lunch counter.

JAVA HOUSE AND HANGOUT
33 Farley's

DOGPATCH DINER
34 Just for You
732 22nd Street

A favorite hash house of both early workers and late sleepers, Just For You moved to grittier pastures in nearby Dogpatch (as the area is known) when Chez Maman moved in. Arienne Landry's southern-tinged cooking (she hails from New Orleans) by way of Mexico serves up everything from beignets to breakfast burritos, cornmeal pancakes to hangtown fry, eggs with everything from Cajun catfish to grits. Add scones hot from the oven and organic fruit and it's the great American breakfast, only better.

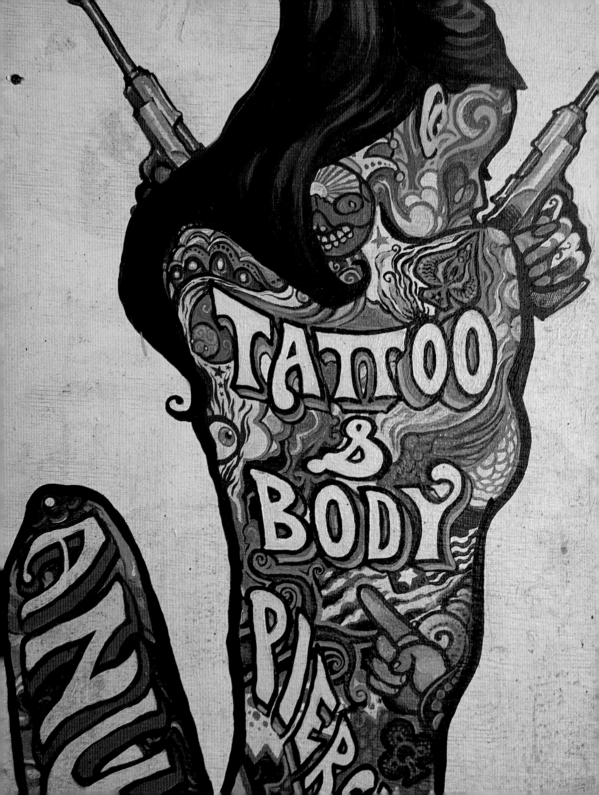

Civic Center
Hayes Valley
Castro
Haight
Golden Gate Park

The most notable thing about Civic Center, the seat of San Francisco's city government, is its phalanx of grand Beaux Arts buildings: City Hall – with a gilded dome modeled on that of St Peter's – the Opera House and the Asian Art Museum, recently given a makeover by Gae Aulenti. There are also some wan plazas that attract the city's more transient residents as well as city workers and attorneys from the courthouse ducking out for a smoke. Civic Center blurs into the Hayes Valley, which was transformed from a den of illicit activity into an indie-chic shopping district when the 1989 earthquake weakened the overhead freeway that had shrouded the area in gloom. Once it came down, shops and bars started popping up like wildflowers, growing increasingly specialized with each passing year. Among other things, you can attend a tasting of California varietals (Amphora Wine Merchant, page 46) or rare sakes (True Sake, page 49), savor a rose-infused crème brulée (Citizen Cake, page 135), pick up a vintage lucite table (Alabaster, page 171) and test-sit a Marc Newson chair (Friend, page 175).

Heading down Gough Street to Market Street takes you past Zuni Café (page 133), which perhaps epitomizes the city's love affair with Cal-Med cuisine, and then it's a stroll up to the Castro district, where rainbow flags unfurl over many of the restored gingerbread Victorians. A gay Mecca since the 1970s, the neighborhood's once working-class Irish population decamped for the suburbs around the time that legions of men started moving in. The Castro Theatre (page 54), designed in 1922 by Timothy Pflueger, is a local landmark and one of the last of the great American movie palaces and a stalwart supporter of classic revivals and independent cinema.

One hill over is another center of alternative living, the Haight Ashbury. A weekend retreat for wealthy San Franciscans in the 19th century, the area became a playground for the acid set by 1967, when Janis Joplin, the Jefferson Airplane and the Grateful Dead all called it home and gave concerts in Golden Gate Park (which commences at the end of Haight Street). But it didn't take long for the Summer of Love to give way to the winter of our discontent, and today's Haight is a somewhat ungainly, patchouli-scented mixture of old head shops and trendy boutiques (such as Kid Robot) sitting cheek-by-jowl on a street patrolled by street urchins (and their dogs). Besides the massive park (page 57), a main draw is the Aub Zam Zam, a Persian hideaway that mixes a mean Martini (page 157). A mile down the road in the more compact Lower Haight, with its gloss of grunge and vitality, high-concept restaurants such as rnm (page 54) have ventured gamely into the cool mix of dive dance clubs, bars, vinyl record shops and alternative galleries.

1 Asian Art Museum

200 Larkin Street

With 15,000 objects spanning 6,000 years of history (including the oldest known Buddha, circa AD 338), this is the largest Asian art collection in the world. Rare and precious objects from forty countries – from tiny carved jades to monumental sculptures, screen paintings, porcelains, lacquers, embroidered textiles, arms and furniture – are shown in rotation. Gae Aulenti transformed this former library with a light touch: an expansive interior skylit courtyard was added to the entrance of the Beaux Arts edifice, while many of the decorative details – the majestic staircase, loggia, vaulted ceilings, travertine finishes – were left intact.

POST-MODERN PATISSERIE

2 Citizen Cake

TWEAKED HABERDASHERY

3 MAC (Modern Appealing Clothing)

LAGOON LOUNGE

4 Jade Bar

650 Gough Street

A cascading, twenty-foot waterfall helps set the aqueous tone, reflected in iridescent blue-green Bisazza tiles, fish tanks, blooming orchids and a koi pond in the subterranean grotto lounge. It's perhaps ironic that this tri-level DJ bar rests on the site of a former Alcoholics Anonymous meeting center, given the well-crafted drinks and special house concoctions (quite reasonably priced), that glow in mermaid colors. The vaguely Asian bites – spring rolls, tuna poke, papaya salad – help slake hunger. And if you're of the male persuasion, don't miss the view through the one-way mirror in the men's room.

CATCH OF THE DAY

5 Hayes Street Grill

320 Hayes Street

Vicolo Pizzeria

201 Ivy Alley

This Hayes Valley fish house (a favorite of the pre-opera crowd) is owned by one of the city's most eloquent food writers, Patricia Unterman, who waxes as passionate about street food as about haute cuisine. The menu is largely based on that day's catch, which is sauteed or tossed onto the mesquite grill and served with a pile of perfect French fries and choice of sauces and salsas. In a corrugated-steel shed behind the restaurant, Vicolo Pizzeria serves its famous cornmeal-crusted pizzas in cast-iron pans and tops them with whole-milk mozzarella, fresh and dried wild mushrooms, house-made sausage and other delights.

LEATHER AND LACE

6 Dark Garden

FRUIT OF THE VINE

7 Hayes and Vine

377 Hayes Street

This neighborhood wine bar in a restored Victorian attracts both professional and lay oenophiles to its serpentine onyx bar and lacquered maple tables. Partners Mark Dirsa and Tony Poer offer 1,200 wines by the bottle and fifty by the glass and ever-changing flights spotlighting specific regions. The balance of home-grown and imports ranges from a scarce 1988 Ridge Montbello from Santa Cruz to an '83 Beaucastel Neuf-du-Pape and a 1990 Burklin-Wolf rare German Riesling. The light menu lists cheeses, pâtés, smoked fish and bread from nearby Citizen Cake.

FOOD AND FLIGHTS

8 Hayes Street

- Absinthe Brasserie & Bar, no. 398
- Arléquin, no. 384B
- Amphora Wine Merchant, no. 384A

First came Absinthe, a plush, Belle Époque-inspired brasserie that begat Arléquin two doors down, a tiny café with a sheltered patio garden that serves kir royales and simple, savory salads and toasted sandwiches – including a Croque Arléquin of ham, Gruyère and Dijon mustard on pain levain that leaves others in the dust. Completing the "A" troika is the Amphora Wine Merchant, where wine director Neil Mechanic curates the few hundred intriguing California and international vintages and facilitates thematic tastings – from Syrahs of the World to dessert wines of Australia.

DESIGNER GOODS

9 Friend

From 1942 to 1984, Pan Am Flight 001 took off from San Francisco and landed in New York 46 hours later by way of Tokyo, Istanbul, London and six other cities. John Sencion and Brad John created this chic little boutique to restore some of that glam to boarding a plane, with *Wallpaper**-worthy luggage, portable backgammon, guidebooks, tangerine leather passport holders, palm-sized gadgets and tiny aromatherapy candles to combat jet lag. Designer Dario Antonioni created a cross between the hull of a 747 and a retro airport lounge, with walnut paneling, Pirelli tiles and powder-blue icons.

Lorn Dittfeld fled a job in advertising to found Propeller, a place for living, breathing designers to show their work. "Eames, Thonet, Naguchi...they're great. But what about the cool stuff with design integrity from our own era?" So he bypassed the canonized mid-century icons and mass-produced pseudo-hip fare to focus on pieces by new talents. You can test-sit Melanie Schnack's rocking Yoga Lounge, find a space-saving magnetic spice rack and pick up one of William Earle's sculpted wood veneer tables, which sell for a relative song.

Simone Signoret once observed that she had no intention of having a face lift, as she'd earned every last wrinkle. Which doesn't stray too far from Russell Pritchard's philosophy regarding furniture: "Always repair, never restore." His shop is filled with gracefully aging Americana, from rust-kissed gliders that once held court on Kansas porches to old Tennessee screen-topped pie coolers and the beautiful Blue Rocket – a 1930s children's carnival ride unearthed in Texas.

Beau Timkin kept a journal of every sake he tasted, "but when I asked my Japanese chef friends where I could buy these amazing *nihonsu*, they just laughed." Thus, after intensive training and accreditation in Japan, Timkin opened the country's first sake-only store in a space that combines the traditional and the hip. Above the riveted stainless-steel double-Dutch doors there's an iguana-green sign with raised transparent letters and a *sugidama* – the ball of cedar that hangs outside breweries in Japan (when the ball has turned brown the sake is ready). Inside are 120 hand-selected varieties, each with a neat description. "Finally," adds Beau, "a use for all those cool sake sets that are gathering dust!"

Suppenküche was conceived as a cross between a Wirtshaus (pub) and a Gasthaus, in the medieval monastic tradition of offering travelers good, fresh fare (and copious amounts of ale) in simple surroundings. The candlelit room has vaulted ceilings, bleached walls scattered with religious icons and communal pine tables where fresh takes on Bavarian classics – crispy potato pancakes, sauerbraten, sauteed venison in red-wine sauce and soup – are accompanied by foaming pints of beer from the homeland. Weekend brunch – cured gravlax, sausage, hearty omelettes, and of course, more beer – is especially popular with the bleached-hair-and-pierced-bits set.

Combining found objects with horticulture, city gardener David Clifton began planting up discarded shoes and propping them atop logs near the potting shed of Alamo Square (also the site of the oft-photographed row of Victorian "painted ladies"). An endless work in progress, it might contain a grass-sprouting sparkly stiletto, a red patent baby shoe full of primroses and a cowboy boot growing onions and pansies.

18 Noon

1637 Market Street

Sheri Sheridan, whose store Swallowtail (page 90) is a photo stylists' clubhouse, took over an immense former antiques store, painted everything white, and banded together with 16 like-minded colleagues, including Pamela Fritz, her partner in the Figurative Design Group. Part design consortium, part showroom, part antique collective, Noon brings together the old (David Allen's Architectural Salvage), the new (London Turner's brand of Palm Springs modernism) and every fabulous thing in between.

ROCOCO RIBBONS
19 Bell'Occhio

8 Brady Street

At the forefront of bespoke bow-tying for years, Bell'Occhio is a self-contained little time-warp that promotes the old metiers – handmade silk millinery flowers, spools of ribbon, amusing boxes (such as a large plastic Honfleur oyster made on antique molds), Parisian face powders, fuchsia silk matador's stockings and other curiosities. It's a tonic, from the esoteric music to the humor with which goods are displayed (one collection of woven straw was called "Paille à la Mode"). Practicing what they procure, they treat every gift to extravagant wrapping.

THE RAW AND THE COOKED
20 Zuni Café

133

CAVIAR BAR
21 Hotel Biron

45 Rose Street

There are no beds at the Hotel Biron (which borrows its name from the edifice that became the Rodin Museum), but there are cushy chairs, couches and scattered tables at which to take wine, caviar and light fare. Located down an alley a few doors from Zuni Café (look for the big "B" and a copper crown rescued from the original Woolworths building), the candlelit wine bar/art gallery exudes an unselfconscious Bohemianism – not so long ago embracing couples would have been screened by a haze of now illicit cigarette smoke. Patrick Panella and Caroline Sanders built the Biron from scratch (the bar was fashioned by wood left over from creating the room-dividing arches) and have compiled a long and careful list of French and up-and-coming California vintages.

SPICE OF LIFE
22 Destino

1815 Market Street

James Schenk's Destino was inspired by his Peruvian mother and a favorite Madrid haunt, the Nuevo Café Barbieri, "which was like my living room." Back in San Francisco, the memories converged into his own brand of nuevo Latino cooking and the neo-colonial vibe of his restaurant, where hand-carved doors open onto a candle-lit room with amber walls and grand mirrors. His menu includes tapa-sized starters (grilled chicken empeñadas with black mint and currants) and larger platos (grilled adobo-rubbed pork loins with chutney, fresh and spicy cebiches), which pair perfectly with the pisco sours, margaritas, and South American and Spanish varietals (noted in a *New York Times* survey of the country's best wine lists).

SWANK SUPPER CLUB
23 Mecca

2029 Market Street

An upper Market hotspot in true New York/LA style, this supper club has an industrial-luxe stainless-steel façade and silky mod interior of velvet drapes, cushy banquettes and – this being the Castro – über-flattering lighting. But there is a culinary imperative to the scene. Chef Stephen Barber marries his Kentucky roots with French methods, producing uptown versions of down home favorites: "14 hour" smokehouse spareribs, duck breast with maple-rhubarb compote and a peppery lobster risotto. Entertainment rotates between people watching at the large oval bar, DJs, jazz vocalists and other amusements.

CHEAP AND CHEERFUL
24 Home

2100 Market Street

Busy, bustling and loud by design, this was an upscale and sophisticated restaurant called John Frank before taking off the tablecloths, hanging up some nostalgic-kitsch décor, and reinventing itself as Home, a packed place to enjoy good cocktails, well-prepared Americana food (Lance Dean Velasquez has earned a passel of rising chef awards), and very easy prices. Also added was a sheltered open-air bar that feels like a perennial party. Nightly specials include fried catfish with braised greens and polenta and braised beef brisket with horseradish creme, and the Sunday brunch scene brings everything from chile verde with tortillas to housemade waffles.

25 Nancy Boy

2319 Market Street

A shower in the window rains continuously into a porcelain tub, a nod to the fresh potions stacked up inside ("tested on boyfriends, not animals"). The range of pharmaceutical-grade botanicals (from hair care to laundry soap) was born in the San Francisco garden of a Nancy Boy founder with a bumper crop of mint and lavender. All the formulations – from light-reflecting pomade to ultramarine night cream to Valencia orange and bergamot bath salts – are filled with hand-distilled herb, fruit and flower extracts that also appeal to Nancy girls.

HOT AND COLD

26 Samovar Tea Lounge

498 Sanchez Street

Old-world charming and new-world cool, Samovar is a lovely place to lounge on fat cushions and bask in the sun streaming through windows while sampling one of the hundred small estate teas and herbal infusions – from organic sencha to premium Darjeeling and chilled Moroccan mint. Opened by London transplant Robert Sandler and designed by Anna Venya, Samovar serves from breakfast to ten at night and cooks up a long menu of tea-compatible small plates – lavender shortbread, veggie samosas, ginger salmon salad, bento boxes, bergamot bread pudding. Saturday evenings a DJ spins jazz, funk and groove from the tea-tasting bar.

CASTRO CROSSROADS

27 Café Flore

146

MEN'S THREADS

28 Rolo

2351 Market Street

It's not surprising that Roland Peters's menswear store Rolo is the only place stocking Mrs Mudd, the new clothing line from actor John Malkovich – the shop has long been the portal by which avant-garde and otherwise interesting collections drop down into San Francisco. While he currently has everything from Levi's Premium to G-Star jeans from Holland, Martine Sitbon, Ted Baker, Rogan denim, Comme des Garçons and Paul Smith, every season brings new twists, and the grooming department is similarly up to snuff.

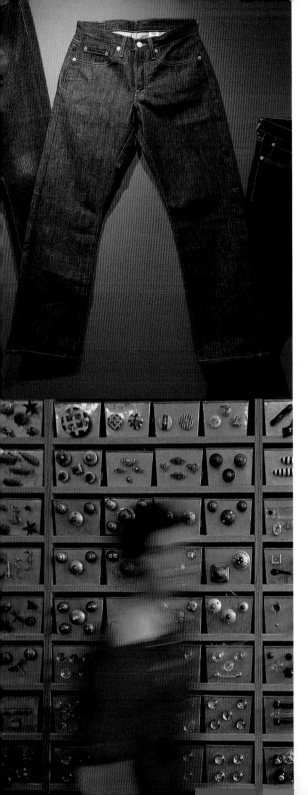

29 Medium Rare Records

2310 Market Street

Filled to the gills with often hard-to-find domestic and import lounge, vocal, soundtrack, show, dance music and curiosities (a CD of nothing but celebrities such as Joan Crawford volubly swearing), tiny Medium Rare Records is run by Michael Williams, who with his business partner estimates about 10,000 CDs in their personal collections alone. "For the store, we follow our tastes," which roam across decades, genres and geography, from new Ibiza to old Italian soundtracks, Shirley Bassey to Les Demoiselles de Rochefort. It's also especially rich in classic soul from the sixties and seventies (Aretha Franklin, Love Unlimited, Gloria Scott), and a burgeoning eighties section is a magnet "for all those folks starting to feel their first twinges of nostalgia." Ouch.

ARTISTIC OPENERS

30 Bauerware

3886 17th Street

"I always wanted to own a hardware store," says interior designer Lou Ann Bauer, whose shop is stacked to the ceiling with every conceivable kind of drawer pull and knob, new and vintage. Rows and rows of galvanized tins hold the work of more than a hundred artisans in materials like ceramic, leather, Bakelite and colored glass, and novelty pulls rendered from poker chips and old mahjong tiles. Some have been fashioned as branches, twigs and acorns; others are machined cleanly out of metal – jewel-like in their minimalism.

FAIRY-TALE FUSION

31 Tallula

4230 18th Street

Harveen Khera's Indian fusion restaurant is in a multilevel Victorian whose tiny rooms are scattered like beads that have fallen off a necklace. Orange and gold walls, candles and stained-glass windows create an effect in concert with the libations, whose descriptions read like riddles from a fairy tale (the kind that either annoy or enchant): "He called. I reminisced. Bittersweet were our kisses. Lemon and licorice." Best bets are the cocktail-friendly chaat: mussels served in a broth of coconut milk, curry and fenugreek, jicama salad sparked with tamarind-ginger, spicy pani puri, frites tossed with garam marsala and served with mango pickle aioli. A coda of cardamom rice pudding cools things down.

32 The Castro Theatre

429 Castro Street

One of the few fantasy movie palaces to escape displacement by a multiplex, the Castro Theatre was designed in 1922 by Timothy Pflueger (who went on to create both Bimbo's (page 155) and the Paramount Theatre (page 104)), and was designated a registered landmark in 1977. A living example of the era's preference for a pastiche of decorative styles, the exterior is reminiscent of a Mexican cathedral (movie house as secular temple), with various Art Déco details and painted sgraffito murals inside. Whether there for a revival (from *Rififi* to *Valley of the Dolls*), special program (*Sing-along Sound of Music*), or festival (International, Gay and Lesbian, Jewish), you'll likely be treated to a live performance on the Mighty Wurlitzer before the opening credits roll.

DJ DEN

33 Nickie's BBQ

460 Haight Street

Nickie's BBQ hasn't cooked ribs in years, but it does serve up a roster of first-class DJs who attract an unusually eclectic mix of writhing bodies to its hardwood dance floor. There's something different every night (Monday's Grateful Dead Jams has been going strong for ten years), but the jewel in the lineup is DJ Cheb i Sabbah, the brilliantly gifted Algerian-born, Paris-bred, Jewish–Berber citizen of the world, and a veteran of the Living Theater in Bordeaux. Every Tuesday, Sabbah takes dancers on a looping journey through ancient and modern Asia, Africa, Arabia and Andalucia, a thrilling musical model for world peace.

DRINKS AND A NOSH

34 Noc Noc

557 Haight Street

Rosamunde Sausage Grill

545 Haight Street

Toronado

547 Haight Street

The Lower Haight (so called to differentiate it from the Haight Ashbury up the road) is San Francisco's tiny slice of the East Village, where a few divey but divine dance clubs (Nickie's BBQ, The Top) share asphalt with boisterous bars, cheap eats and stylish restaurants such as rnm. One could kick off an evening with a sake cocktail at the Noc Noc, a shadowy lounge that feels like a cross between

Mad Max and Alice in Wonderland. When feeling peckish, a wander to the Rosamunde Sausage Grill reveals an array of bun-destined delicacies – Knockwurst, Bratwurst, Provençal, duck with cherries, seafood – and condiments from sauteed onions to chili. This alcohol-absorbing fare may then be carted to riotous Toronado next door, whose taps dispense dozens of lagers and ales under the watchful eye of the stuffed deer.

SLICK EATS

35 rnm

598 Haight Street

A slick, high-design restaurant sitting on a block better known for dark dive bars and roving skate punks – rnm is a diamond in the rough. After previous stints at Postrio and Globe, Justine Miner (who named the restaurant to honor her late father) turns out small plates with a passion for organic ingredients that borders on fetishism. Cucumber gazpacho gets a hit of Meyer lemon and a morsel of Dungeness crab, a sizzling pizza is topped with grilled radicchio, sushi-grade ahi is trussed up on roasted garlic toast with a savory salad of potatoes, tomatoes and olives, and a rack of Australian lamb rests on mint and parmesan farro – all of which can be enjoyed at tables, at the bar, or on the couch in the swanky, low-lit mezzanine.

COCKTAILS IN THE CASBAH

36 Persian Aub Zam Zam

PERPETUAL PLAYLIST

37 Amoeba Music

1855 Haight Street

Every nook of this former bowling alley (and largest indie record store in the country) is filled with new and used music in all its iterations – vinyl, CDs, 78s, tapes, DVDs, even 8-tracks. But more important to both casual browsers and music geeks is the breadth of the selection – jazz, rock, soul, international folk, roots, electronica, classical – and the staff, who have heard of every obscure thing you can throw at them and know where to find it. Some people come not to buy, sell or trade, but to enjoy free in-store appearances by local and touring bands (Moby, Richard Thompson, Karsh Kale, the White Stripes).

38 Golden Gate Park

Bordered by Stanyan Street, Fulton Street, the Great Highway and Lincoln Way

Beach Chalet

1000 Great Highway

Hosting a million trees, a bison paddock, Shakespeare garden, tulip garden, polo fields, crystal palace, lake for boating and sundry museums, Golden Gate Park is the literal interpretation of the California dream – nature tamed within wide-open spaces, a smattering of culture and room for rollerblading – albeit one truncated by roads and frequently shrouded in fog. The greensward stretches 1,013 acres, from the tip to the Haight Ashbury to the western coastline, and was originally designed to shield residents from harsh winds and horse-and-buggy traffic. Among indoor attractions under construction are the California Academy of Sciences, which houses an aquarium, planetarium and natural history exhibits (replete with simulated earthquake), and de Young Museum, currently undergoing a modernist makeover by Swiss architects Herzog & de Meuron. The Conservatory of flowers, modeled after the Palm House at Kew Gardens (and smashed in hurricane-like storms), recently reopened amidst much pomp, sheltering a hundred-year-old imperial philodendron and pollination exhibit starring 800 live butterflies. Outdoors, the Strybing Arboretum supports 7,500 species on seventy acres of horticultural bliss. And the Japanese Tea Garden's paths, ponds and tiny footbridges offer both a spot for reflection and a refreshing cuppa with cookies. For those more inclined towards beer and a view, the historic Beach Chalet restaurant, built in 1926 by architect Willis Polk as a lounge and changing area, overlooks the pounding Pacific on the west end of the park and houses Lucien Labaudt's WPA-era murals of San Franciscans engaged in seaside leisure.

Financial District
Telegraph Hill
North Beach
Chinatown

If there is a "quintessential" San Francisco — that is, an area so rife with iconic signifiers that it could be identified by a Martian — it surely resides within this patchwork of neighborhoods. But unlike, say, Fisherman's Wharf, each also has a life apart from its postcard persona and offers some of the best walking — and drinking — in the city.

The soaring spire of the Transamerica Pyramid (page 65), the solar plexus of the Financial District, may be as much a cliché as the cable cars that come rumbling down California Street, but the lovely park of redwood trees tucked beside it is unknown even to many locals. Decorous antique stores now occupy the brick buildings of nearby Jackson Square (bounded by Washington, Kearny, Jackson and Pacific), the only surviving pre-Victorian-style area, whose brothels and raucous saloons once serviced the gold-mad frontier boomtown.

Another Gold Rush by-product is Chinatown, whose original inhabitants fled famine and wars to toil in the mines and then on the railroads. One of the most densely populated areas in the country, its history is deftly traced at the Chinese Historical Society Museum (page 71) and felt in the bustling streets off the Grant Avenue strip of curio stores, especially on market days when shoppers jostle amidst the produce, live poultry and tanks of fish. Down side streets tiny storefronts contain herbalists, bakeries and jook joints, and religious shrines are filled with offerings and incense. A good place to soak up the atmosphere is over a cup of Dragon Well at the Imperial Tea Court (page 149), or stronger stuff at Li Po (page 156), reputed to be a former opium den.

In North Beach, where the daytime beverage of choice is espresso, gentrification has never quite conquered the Bohemian spirit that attracted the Beats, who grooved on the good cheap food and wine they found in the Little Italy settled by fishermen from Genoa. The North Beach of the imagination exists in the sidewalk cafes, pastry shops and eccentric bars; in jewel-like restaurants like Da Flora (page 140), and in the dreamy Hotel Bohème (page 124) — if perhaps not in the Broadway strip clubs. The conscience of the neighborhood is City Lights Booksellers (page 168), while the heart is Washington Square, where older Italians gossip on benches as their Chinese counterparts practice tai chi on the grass.

Crowned by Coit Tower, Telegraph Hill Rises straight up from North Beach, but is most magically approached via the Filbert Steps on the other side (page 62). Rich in foliage and cats, the path leads past charming Victorian cottages and over the only wood-plank street left in San Francisco — a survivor of the earthquake and fire that erased so much of this city's early history.

SLEEPING AT THE WATER'S EDGE
1 Hotel Griffon

FOOD MECCA
2 Ferry Building

ORGANICALLY GROWN
3 Farmers' Market

FRESH FUSION
4 Slanted Door

CANDY COUTURIER
5 Recchiuti Confections

GOLD RUSH RELIC
6 Tadich Grill
240 California Street

San Francisco's oldest restaurant was opened as a coffee stand in 1849 by three Croatian immigrants. The clubby, wood interior with linen-cloaked tables and white-tiled floor still channels the Gold Rush days, and the food is similarly of a distant era. Although Tadich was the first restaurant to grill fish over mesquite charcoal, much of the fare is far from nouvelle, with lobster Newburg, creamed spinach and oyster stew listed on the menu with turn-of-the-century typesetting. From glancing around the room you might surmise that the house wine is ice-cold Martinis, straight up with an olive.

RUSTIC CHIC
7 Globe
290 Pacific Avenue

Serving dinner until 1 am, Globe is a favored haunt of local chefs looking to relax in this former livery stable with exposed brick walls covered with splashy paintings. Executive chef Joseph Manzare used to cook with Wolfgang Puck, and the menu leans toward large, rustic preparations served in big ceramic bowls and tasty twists on American staples – such as the macaroni and cheese prepared with Tillamook cheddar and thick bucatini pasta and a T-bone steak presented on a pedestal with grilled onions and a soulful helping of potatoes gratin.

CRAFTED CAFÉ
8 Café de Stijl
1 Union Street

Architect Nilus de Matran designed the interior of his café and named it in homage to the Mondrian-led art movement. The work of his wife, graphic designer Jennifer Morla, is displayed on the brick walls, rusted steel letters are embedded in the concrete floor, and a ceramicist was commissioned to make the black and white plates and latte bowls. On fair days, a sunny sidewalk table is the place to enjoy buttermilk waffles with fruit, fresh panini, soups, composed salads and specials such as curry chicken.

STAIRWAY TO HEAVEN
9 Filbert Steps
Begins on Sansome Street, goes up to Telegraph Hill

There are many ways to get to Coit Tower, but none as satisfying as climbing the (187) Filbert Steps that rise in three sections all the way from Sansome Street. It's a hike, but with each step the city recedes and one becomes surrounded with lush foliage, Victorian cottages, birdsong, and sometimes one of the flocks of wild green parrots that roam the city. The route leads you past the wondrous Grace Marchant gardens and Napier Lane, the last wood-plank street in the city, and when you reach the summit the views of Alcatraz and Angel Island feel entirely earned.

UPWARDLY MOBILE
10 Coit Tower
1 Telegraph Hill

Various stories exist to account for Lillie Hitchcock Coit's obsession with firemen, but whether the eccentric philanthropist was saved from a blaze as a child or simply liked men in uniform, she left a chunk of her fortune to build this 1933 cement monument atop Telegraph Hill to the city's firefighters. (That it was designed to resemble a fire hose is pure folklore.) An elevator takes you to an observation deck in the turret, but the view in the lobby is just as compelling. The socialist–realist WPA murals painted by local artists during the Depression were supervised by Diego Rivera and document both the richness of California's natural resources and the struggles of its workers (depicted as rather buff). At the time, the frescoes ruffled feathers with their supposedly leftist leanings and a hammer and sickle were censored before the unveiling.

WEST-COAST BASQUE
11 Piperade

140

WATER, WATER EVERYWHERE
12 Tru
750 Kearny Street

Craig Fossella knows a few things about spas, having served as global spa director for Blissworld. His first solo venture is a modern, airy day spa designed by Chris Kofitsas with bamboo floors and lots of natural light nestled into an unlikely location off the lobby of the Holiday Inn, Chinatown. But the treatments are transporting, from massages that incorporate colored light therapy (shades of Josef Albers), Moji-Toe pedicures that use fresh mint and lime, and delicious face and body treatments – such as Pulp Fiction Polish, which applies fresh fruit pulp, sweet almond oil, shea butter, sugar and grapefruit essential oil to get back the glow. Wet treatments take place in the Rainforest Room, a jungle retreat with rock walls, tropical rain, piped-in African beats and a waterfall for rinsing off the delicious concoctions that have been slathered onto skin and scalp.

EARTH AND SKY
13 Transamerica Pyramid and Redwood Park
600 Montgomery Street

Provoking outrage when it went up in 1972, the image of William Pereira's 853-foot building (the city's tallest) jutting into the skyline has mellowed into an icon. Less known is the park that rests beside it, an unexpected retreat planted with redwoods in the heart of the financial district. Within the park is a commemorative plaque to two of the city's notable citizens, Bummer and Lazarus, stray dogs who followed "Mad Hatter" Emperor Norton (the self-declared Emperor of the United States) around town until his death in 1880. Among Norton's many decrees was making use of "the abominable word 'Frisco' punishable by the sum of $25."

BUILDERS' ARTS
14 William K. Stout Architectural Books
804 Montgomery Street

At architect and publisher William Stout's multilevel bookstore, that Harry Potter chap is nowhere in sight. Instead, current chart-toppers include *IDEO Method Cards: 51 Ways to Inspire Design*, from the Bay Area-based product design firm, and a monograph on Eichler, the pioneering developer who hired progressive architects to create sleek "California style" modernist homes, of which there are many local examples. Despite the hometown connections, there's nothing provincial about the store, which is something of a designer's Mecca. Manager Alan Silver recalls a clutch of Spanish architects who came in search of a slip-cased book on Richard Neutra: "They cleaned us out – despite the fact that the book was $120 and written in Italian!"

ZEN SPACE
15 Japonesque Gallery

173

PERFECT ESPRESSO
16 Thomas E. Cara Ltd
517 Pacific Avenue

Sitting between the rococo antique shops of Jackson Square and the Kartell showroom is a store that reflects the monomania of its founder, a fourth-generation North Beach native. Stationed in Italy during the War, Thomas E. Cara brought back the first espresso machine west of the Mississippi – a huge, gas-fired, eagle-crowned affair that watches over the gleaming modern La Pavoni and Riviera machines and his collection of vintage java brewers. Running the shop is son Christopher, who considers espresso-making a "meditative ritual," thus the bias for manual models. And because a cup is only as good as the beans, he also sells their top-secret blend, the recipe for which Cara senior brought back from Naples (and ships to customers as far as France).

AUTEUR CAFÉ
17 Café Niebaum-Coppola
916 Kearny Street

Thirty years ago, Francis Ford Coppola drafted the script to "The Godfather" in the historic, copper-clad Sentina [Sentinol] Building, a survivor of the 1906 'quake. Today, his production company, American Zoetrope, occupies the upper floors of the wedge-shaped building, while his ground-floor café serves rustic fare such as wood-fired blistered pizzas, pastas and Argentine tapas called *picadas* (marinated anchovies, olive pâté, garlic sausage), with a heated terrace for al fresco dining. The wine list draws liberally from the Niebaum-Coppola Napa winery (bottles available for purchase) and if you show up the second Tuesday of the month you'll be treated to "Live Story," Zoetrope's popular series featuring big-name actors reading short stories and plays.

18 Tosca Café

19 Specs' Twelve Adler Museum Café
12 Adler Place

Known for his talent at spinning a yarn, Specs Simmons opened his saloon down an alley off Columbus Street in 1968, the final incarnation of a former speakeasy and Chinese joss house. He welcomed all kinds – writers, longshoremen, Irish musicians, American activists – a lassiez-faire attitude that extends to the décor of ancient masks, Spanish Civil War posters, taxidermy (including a stuffed puffin and a mongoose battling a cobra) and all manner of flotsam brought back by his seafaring friends. The music is similarly eclectic – ranging from Irish to Klezmer. And Specs' also seems to understand that drink sometimes requires food, with a menu that consists exclusively of saltine crackers and a generous slab of gouda.

POETS AND POSEURS
20 Vesuvio
255 Columbus Avenue

Vesuvio has been a watering hole for jazz musicians, poets (such as Dylan Thomas) and hangers-on since 1948, and has the dusty memorabilia to prove it. One legend has Jack Kerouac stepping in for a quick one on his way to Big Sur to meet up with Henry Miller, but never quite making it thanks to an endless round of cocktails (he did, however, phone every hour). These days you're more likely to find professionals and tourists packed in the downstairs bar, while seasoned regulars huddle upstairs in the darker, pub-like area, scribbling and philosophizing into the night.

BEAT BOOKS
21 City Lights Bookseller & Publisher

LEFT-BANK STYLE
22 Hotel Bohème

NIGHT IN VENICE
23 Da Flora

CAFÉ SOCIETY
24 Mario's Bohemian Cigar Store
566 Columbus Avenue

Founded as a cigar shop by Mario Crismani and his wife, Liliana, Mario's evolved into a café and then a fixture, with locals dropping in to play cards, talk politics and exchange the gossip swirling round Washington Square. You'll still find an assortment of regulars and eccentrics (not mutually exclusive) seated at one of the six tables or bellied up to the wood counter sipping espresso or eating Mario's famous focaccia sandwiches – such as breaded eggplant with Swiss cheese, bell peppers and marinara or hot meatball with grilled onions – transformed into melting wonders in the counter-top Baker's Pride oven.

HOT FOCACCIA
25 Liguria Bakery
1700 Stockton Street

At Liguria, they do one thing extremely well. And when they sell out of it, they close. You can smell this tiny storefront focacceria just off Washington Square before you see it. Founded in 1911 by three brothers from Genoa, it's run by George Soracco, the son of one of the founders, and his two children. Choose plain, tomato, garlic, raisin or scallion-topped flatbread and they cut it in half, wrap it in wax paper and tie it up with string, although it's hard to get very far without tearing into it.

SWEET MORSELS
26 XOX Truffles
754 Columbus Avenue

You could walk past this tiny shop and not realize that it produces some of the most esteemed chocolates in America. Jean-Marc Gorce and his wife, Casima, make their artisanal goods here and ship them all over the world. Unlike the steroid-bulked truffles that dominate some confection cases, it takes about eighty of these irregularly shaped morsels to make up a pound. They come dusted with cocoa or coated with coffee crunch, hazelnut, white chocolate or coconut, in an array of intense *parfums* – including Earl Grey, cognac, crème de menthe, bitter orange and a melting burnt caramel ganache. As this is California, there are also vegan options, from French Roast to rum coco.

"Quirky," "eccentric," "wildly decorative," are qualities that excite Conor Fennessy, who has one of the most eclectic-yet-clean collections around. The Dublin-born interior designer combs estate sales and auctions for objects with scale, character and spice. A red lacquered Paul Frankl table designed for Brown Saltman of California has a place by "Mammy," a 70-year-old papier mâché Mardi Gras mask from New Orleans, and an African stool with doves carved on its base harmonizes with the jazzy Prouvé-like table with stiletto legs and ebonized ends. Harder to categorize is a huge lightning bolt, whose wood grain bleeds beautifully through the paint.

Long before it was *de rigueur* to decorate a square inch or two of one's anatomy with ink, tattoo legend Lyle Tuttle was transforming the field from an exercise in tracing hearts and anchors into a vehicle for artistic expression. Tuttle has retired, but his legacy lives on at this parlor and mini-museum run by his former apprentice, Tanja Nixx, a German artist who became fascinated with body adornment after traveling through Africa and Asia. She has archives of designs or can help you translate an original vision onto the body part of your choice.

Lighter than air, Alla Prima's bras, bustiers, panties and camis can exert a paradoxically strong reaction on their beholders. There are sporty numbers and full-on "Belle de Jour" froth – embellished bits of silk and lace in colors ranging from basic black to cassis, mint and Fanta orange by the likes of La Perla, Alberta Ferretti, Chantal Thomas, Aubade, Cosabella and Leigh Bantivoglio – some of whose flirty slip dresses are (barely) street legal. The shop at 539 Hayes Street has a mezzanine devoted to swimwear, and owner Yolaida Duran is a fiend about fit – using her trusty tape measure to flatter gamines and bombshells alike.

Like anybody with a true calling, Bill Haskell found his at a tender age, when he rescued a pair of Victorian glass domes from his parents' New Jersey basement. Life has been one big salvage operation ever since, with Aria his brilliant repository of "antiques, art, funk and junk," displaying the bounty of Haskell's foraging at home and abroad: articulated artist models, writing ephemera, santos figures, vintage Tour de France and boxing photos, toile-mounted maps, opera glasses, Bakelite boxes, antique wood California furniture, paintings, display mannequins and heaps of rescued treasures.

Buckets are filled with fresh and seasonal flowers – lilacs, heirloom sweet peas that smell intoxicating and spray roses. The rest of the store is a curio cabinet of sailors' valentines – anchors and treasure boxes studded with seashells – gothic iron crosses, tableaux vivants rendered from roadkill (imagine *Hamlet* as enacted by mice), and essentials such as faux taxidermied ravens that add a dash of Edward Gorey charm to any abode.

LIGHTER THAN AIR
35 Café Jacqueline
1454 Grant Avenue

After twenty years, the number of eggs that Jacqueline Margulis has gone through at her painfully romantic, low-lit little café would probably stretch from North Beach to the moon. Because apart from some soups and salads, chez Jacqueline is all about the art of the soufflé, in iterations from the basic (Gruyère) to the more involved (asparagus and salmon topped with thin shreds of lemon, a melange of wild mushrooms), and the downright decadent (lobster, black truffle). Some diners come later in the hope of finding a table and diving, à deux or trois, into a molten yet airy bittersweet chocolate, strawberry or raspberry concoction – cholesterol as aphrodisiac.

CHINESE MASTER
36 Jai Yun

NIGHT OWLS' BANQUET
37 Yuet Lee Seafood Restaurant
1300 Stockton Street

At this Hong Kong–style restaurant, the dishes keep coming until three in the morning, by which point the day-glo color scheme and fluorescent lighting are beside the point. What is the point are the plates of pepper and salt roast prawns, clams with pepper and black bean sauce, whole steamed catfish and pan-fried noodles with sturgeon, all delivered with brisk but friendly efficiency. Many of the delicacies that other restaurants post in Chinese are in English, so you can be as adventurous as you like without feeling left out. The menu (which also features many non-oceangoing items and a host of noodle options) offers clay pots of abalone with duck feet, aromatic beef tripe, oyster and roast pork with ginger, and seasonal specials such as live Boston lobster and sautéed frog legs.

THE WAY OF TEA
38 Imperial Tea Court

STYLISH CHILL SPACE
39 Rosewood

Follow the scent of wafting incense as you enter the century-old building, make your way past the mah-jongg parlor and up to the colorful shrine dedicated to the Queen of the Heavens and Goddess of the Seven Seas. In this brightly painted sanctuary, lanterns hang from the ceiling, and oranges and other tributes are arrayed on altars where colorful paper "money" is burned as offerings. In Chinatown, it's the alleys that teem with back-street activity, and Waverly Place, known as the "street of painted balconies," is itself worth a visit, as is nearby Ross, the area's oldest alley. Once known for its opium dens and gambling joints, Ross is today featured in film shoots (*Indiana Jones and the Temple of Doom*) and is home to the Sam Bo Trading Company and the Golden Gate Fortune Cookie Factory, where one can observe the prescient pastries being made.

TRACING THE PAST
42 Chinese Historical Society of America
965 Clay Street

A brick building designed by Julia Morgan (perhaps better known for Hearst Castle) houses one of the country's largest collections of Chinese–American artifacts, from an antique Buddhist altar to opium pipes and posters for *Chan Is Missing*. On permanent exhibit, "The Chinese of America: Toward a More Perfect Union" traces the history of the Chinese in the United States (by 1882, the same year the racist Chinese Exclusion Act was passed, 75 percent of the agricultural workforce in California was Chinese). The Daniel Ching Collection shows a fraction of the nearly 10,000 items he amassed of often stereotypical images on postcards, books, sheet music, political cartoons, toys and more, and one gallery is dedicated to contemporary artists.

Pacific Heights
Presidio Heights
The Presidio
Richmond

Old and new money intermingle in the large swath of real estate known as Pacific Heights, whose Victorian and Edwardian mansions embellished with architectural and botanical flourishes – from fairy-tale turrets to fanciful topiary – sit in calm repose on leafy streets poised to offer glimpses of the alternatively blue and steel grey bay beyond. The Haas-Lilienthal House – the only Queen Anne-style wooden Victorian open to the public – offers a well-preserved look at how the other half used to live (page 79), while many of the neighborhood's current denizens get their needs met along Fillmore Street between Bush and Jackson – a row of semi-precious shops and charming restaurants (Vivande Porta Via, page 79; Chez Nous, page 77) interspersed with interlopers such as Starbucks. A half-dozen thrift and vintage stores filled with trophy label donations by the local swells make the strip a happy hunting ground, and there are two sprawling and well-tended parks: woodsy Lafayette (near the Haas-Lilienthal House) and the multi-terraced Alta Plaza (a block off Fillmore), with its bird's-eye views of the surrounding manmade and natural wonders.

Turning west off Fillmore onto Sacramento or Clay guides you towards Presidio Heights, an even tonier enclave endowed with many more recherché ways of spending money, not to mention a 1,500-acre backyard in the form of the Presidio, whose woods, meadows and beaches used to belong to the military but now are open to the people. Among the new civilian tenants is Lucas Film and local treasure Andrew Hoyem, whose Arion Press (page 83) creates exquisite handwrought limited editions of everything from Milton's *Paradise Lost* to Italo Calvino's *Invisible Cities*.

Continuing west one eventually arrives in the Richmond, a fog-laced residential district off most tourist maps, whose considerable Chinese, Vietnamese, Korean and Japanese population supports numerous Asian grocers, herbalists, restaurants and packed dim sum teahouses, especially along Geary and bustling Clement Street (Ton Kiang being among the best). These avenues are broken up by tiny gems like Pizzetta 211 (page 134) and eventually lead to beaches – such as pretty, sheltered China Beach (off 26th Avenue, in Sea Cliff), named for the Chinese fishermen who camped on its shores in the 19th century. Farther down is Lincoln Park, home to the Palace of the Legion of Honor (page 84), whose Achenbach Collection is the largest gathering of graphic prints in the western United States. A slightly obscured path behind the museum joins up with the Coastal Trail, which extends both to the Golden Gate Bridge and the eerie ruins of the old Sutro Baths (which may be recalled from the film *Harold and Maude*), a Victorian playground with six fresh- and saltwater pools under a soaring glass dome that was abandoned and finally burned.

OLD SCHOOL ADIDAS

1 Harputs

1527 Fillmore Street

Gus Harput is very old-school, at least when it comes to Adidas. It helps that his dad and uncle, who founded the store, never held a sale. "Instead, they just shoved all the unsold stuff into boxes and tossed 'em in the basement – where they've slowly appreciated like fine wine sitting in the cellar!" Today, those original track shoes and warm-up suits from the sixties, seventies and eighties mingle with newer models that sell for considerably less. There are a few styles from Nike and Asics, but this is really a temple to Adidas, some even imported from Milan and Tokyo. Gus is currently working to transform the space next door into a club – just the place to wear that Run-DMC track suit.

HIGH VICTORIANA

2 Hotel Majestic

112

ELEVATING THE FOOT

3 Paolo

1971 Sutter Street

His deerskin split-toe ankle boot with perforated detail would pair nicely with Comme des Garçons, while high boots with lace-up corset backing are more Versace-friendly. Paolo Iantorno designs two collections a year and has them handcrafted in Italy from skins both domestic and exotic. While the décor of his stores (the other resides in the Hayes Valley) veers toward fountains and trompe l'oeil frescoes, the shoes are modern and sexy – from antiqued kidskin low-heeled loafers to strappy python sandals with lethal metal stilettos. Designs for men are suitable for everyone from dandies (two-toned cap-toe boots with spats) to club cowboys and business types craving an edge.

FOOD FOR THE SOUL

4 Bay Bread Boulangerie

2325 Pine Street

Chez Nous

1911 Fillmore Street

Pascal Rigo's ever-expanding collection of cafés and restaurants is now large enough to constitute an empire, and thus far he appears to have a Midas touch. At his artisanal boulangerie/patisserie, the rustic breads are baked with organic flour in *pavailler* ovens imported from France, and all the cakes, tarts and pastries are sweet without being cloying. Within shouting distance of Bay Bread is perpetually packed Chez Nous. The pan-Mediterranean small plates are scaled to fit prevailing culinary preferences as well as the tiny tables, and channel the entire seaside region – from Italy, Spain and France to Greece, Turkey and Morocco – without feeling schizophrenic. The menu changes with the seasons, but mainstays include baby lamb chops dusted with lavender salt, housemade gnocchi, spinach sautéed with raisins and toasted pignoli, crispy salty divine frites and a salad of grilled calamari, mandarins and greens. The no-reservation policy results in some sidewalk heel-cooling (especially at dinner), but has the advantage of encouraging spontaneity.

PLAYING DRESS UP

5 Heather

2408 Fillmore Street

Cielo

2225 Fillmore Street

While clothing boutiques are far from an endangered species on this high-end street, there aren't many that stand out from the pack. Heather Frazier's cozy space is a refuge for hand-selected pieces by small designers, pulled together by a shared predilection for rich color, pattern and playfulness. Alpina Bwana's embroidered cotton and linen dresses and tunics, Neisha Crosland's sarongs, scarves, hats and bags; the Nuala line of yoga streetwear conceived by Christy Turlington for Puma, and whimsical paper goods are pretty without being precious. Down the street at Cielo, there's a bias towards Belgians – with Dries Van Noten's dream-inspired creations and Ann Demeulemeester's streamlined separates for angst-addled urban poets – including all the shawls, shoes and attendant bags.

NEWS BREAK

6 Juicy News

2453 Fillmore Street

Dispensing both print and potables, this juice and smoothy bar is stocked with oranges and grapefruits as well as design books, boatloads of glossy magazines and international newspapers, which you peruse to the sound of the whirring blender. It's worth a detour just for the frothy concoction of chocolate frozen yogurt, bananas, cinnamon and milk known as the Chocolatier.

Founded by three women – experts in yoga, bodywork and esthetics – International Orange's white-and-dark wood minimalist environment is more evocative of a modern gallery than an ashram. The furniture in the intimate lounge area is in the mode of sculptor Donald Judd, and details such as aromatic flowers that float below the face cradle of massage tables, bowls of chocolate truffles, floor-to-ceiling windows in the yoga studio and a redwood sundeck for relaxing after an Astanga workout, hot stone massage, or lavender-tangerine salt rub make this a place to install oneself for the day.

At the second Kiehl's apothecary to open in 151 years (the East Village flagship set up in 1851), pharmacy cabinets proffer hundreds of botanically based beauty potions – French rose bath foam, honey-almond face scrub, a lip balm that ends up on every model's "desert island" list – in oft-imitated packaging that favors information over trendy graphics. (The company also declined to test on animals or add colorants long before either practice became chic.) There are copious samples, freely given, and even a little something for your horse: a new Equine grooming line was created for the beloved pony of Nicoletta Heidegger, great-granddaughter of the Kiehl's family founder.

Carlo Middione, the proprietor of this gastronomia/ trattoria/groceria, is descended from generations of Sicilian restaurateurs, and his classic *Food of Southern Italy* received what is now known as the (rather prestigious) James Beard Award. While Middione is a slow-food evangelist, half his establishment consists of an immense deli case where cooked-from-scratch comestibles (frittata with housemade sausage, roasted chicken, tortas) are ready to take away. Like all good neighborhood haunts, Vivande has its share of lunch and dinner regulars, who settle into the cozy, brick-walled dining area for Ligurian seafood stew, risotto ai funghi and breast of chicken seared under a brick and escorted with white beans and spinach. Unlike at the most of the trendy coffee joints nearby, the espresso tastes like the nectar of gods that it is.

For all its fascination with Victoriana, San Francisco has but one private historic home open to the public (three days per week). It was designed in 1886 by architect Peter Schmidt for a Baravian émigré named William Haas, passed to Haas' daughter Alice Lilienthal, and stayed in the family until 1972. Built in the Queen Anne style, with elaborate wooden gables, circular corner tower and ornamentation, it's chock full of original furnishings and artifacts (the kitchen is most fascinating) though actually rather modest when compared with mansions that surrounded it until the great fire of 1906.

13 Lion Pub

2062 Divisadero Street

No sign marks this hideaway, but it's impossible to walk past the twinkling Christmas lights and imposing wooden door without taking pause. Founded in the 1980s as a discreet gay bar for Pac Heights professionals, Lion Pub has evolved into more of a social free-for-all. A roaring fire and hot toddy selection make it a cozy midwinter refuge, while on more temperate nights bartenders mix speciality cocktails made with freshly squeezed juices. Intimate tables and a back lounge allow for conversation over red flickering candles, an ideal spot to get to know that special someone you've just met.

RIOT OF COLOR

14 The Bar

340 Presidio Avenue

Fetish

344 Presidio Avenue

Men like The Bar for its comfortable couches, piles of magazines and espresso bar serving complimentary java, which gives women time to swan around in floaty numbers by Ghost and Gharani Strok, embroidered silk dresses by Megan Park, jeans du jour and cardigans printed with old-fashioned florals and stripes by Japan's Antipast. The shop is hard to miss, as the door is painted the bright red of a London phone box. Next door, Fetish stocks the kind of footwear favored by the *Sex and the City* quartet, which is to say lots of straps and precarious heels (hence the name).

HOUSE PROUD

15 Sue Fisher King

3067 Sacramento Street

Sue Fisher King is the sort of place you might find a tilting vase by Christian Tortu, ceramics with subtle glazes by American potter Steve Stewart, hand-blown glass by Simon Pearce (an Irish artist who makes his home stateside), bone-handled silverware, and any number of ways to dress a table or bed. It's also a particular fave of photo stylists, who can always find the exact shade of pale persimmon or muddled mint required to complete a shot.

CHERRY-PICKED FURNISHINGS

16 March

3075 Sacramento Street

Sam Hamilton and Mark Cunningham met while working for Ralph Lauren in New York in assorted creative capacities. Their furniture store, March, could not be further from either the Gatsbyesque nostalgia of their former employer or the recherché antiques shops that line Sacramento Street like dowager aunts. Whether vintage or newly commissioned, everything has clean, spare lines and good bones – from an 18th-century walnut bench to French welding screens, a steel-and-glass dining table from the 1970s and the over-scaled pottery and stone vessels, some old and some being made at this very moment.

HARD-TO-FIND DESIGNERS

17 Susan

3685 Sacramento Street

The Grocery Store

3625 Sacramento Street

If there's a quasi-eccentric but rarefied label you can't find anywhere, odds are good it's hanging at Susan. A case in point is Project Alabama, the hand-quilted cotton couture pieces designed by New York textile artist Natalie Chanin and stitched by sewing circles back in her native Florence (Alabama, that is). Susan is also the only local store stocking Comme des Garçons for women, including Junya Watanabe's surreal fairy-tale pieces. Sportier garb down at The Grocery Store includes Yohji's diffusion line, Maharishi, Easton Pearson and enough designer denim for Christo to wrap the Bay Bridge.

MATERIAL WORLD

18 Satin Moon Fabrics

32 Clement Street

Bolt upon bolt of mind-blowing fabrics are tucked into every nook and cranny, each hand-selected by Alice and Susan Miyamoto. The sisters have maintained this textile jewelbox for thirty years and filled it with mid-century geometrics, vintage reproduction cotton prints, old-world chenilles, Indian voiles, embroidered silks, crushed velvets, Japanese rayon prints, patterns appropriate for children's rooms, and drawers full of horn, glass and shell buttons. Even those who can't sew a stitch come to grab a few yards for one-off shawls, tablecloths and bedspreads.

19 The Presidio

Entrances on Presidio Boulevard, West Pacific Avenue,
Lyon Street and Marine Drive

A good example of the benefits of beating swords into
plowshares, these 1,480 acres of pristine land at the city's
northern tip were converted from military use into a
National Park in 1994, after 220 years as a military post
under the flags of Spain, Mexico and the United States. Now
part of the Golden Gate National Recreation Area, the
Presidio boasts historical buildings – from Civil War
mansions to turn-of-the-century barracks – coastal defense
fortifications, a quirky pet cemetery, saltwater marshes,
forests, beaches, native plant habitats, hiking and biking
trails and views, views, views. While the area is accessible
from different neighborhoods, the gate on Presidio Avenue
and Jackson Street takes you from the modern world
directly into mist-shrouded woods – like entering a fairy
tale. Maps are available at visitor centers in the park.

BOOKMAKERS' ART

20 The Arion Press

1802 Hays Street

Andrew Hoyem is a celebrated man of (hand-set) letters,
and the founder of Arion Press, which has created limited
editions of everything from Czeslaw Milosz to Raymond
Chandler, all illustrated with specially commissioned
artwork. When Arion was evicted from its South of Market
digs during the dot-com heyday, it was designated an
"irreplaceable cultural treasure" and moved to a former
steam plant on the Presidio's southern edge, which also
houses twelve presses and a type foundry. The library
exhibits such collector's items as the Hoyem-designed
Moby Dick with woodcuts by Barry Moser, whose handset
type is printed on handmade blue paper with a whale
watermark and bound in blue goatskin, and John
Ashbery's poem "Reflections in a Convex Mirror," with
lithographs by Willem de Kooning and Jasper Johns,
encased in a round metal canister topped with a convex
mirror. Arion's books range, like Hoyem's curiosity, all over
the map – from Elias Canetti (*The Voices of Marrakesh*) to
Tom Stoppard (*Arcadia*), *Paradise Lost* to *Ulysses* (illustrated
by Robert Motherwell), Henry Roth to Hoyem's old pal
Richard Brautigan, whose *Trout Fishing in America* was
illustrated by Wayne Thiebaud. In 2000, Arion took on
the mother of all books, the Bible, which is still being
bound – it takes a day to handstitch each behometh.

RUSTIC FARE
21 Desiree
39 Mesa Street, Suite 107

When her marriage ended, chef Annie Gingrass (veteran of Spago in Los Angeles and Postrio in San Francisco), left her own extremely upscale restaurant, Hawthorne Lane, to open this sweet, sunny café in the Presidio's San Francisco Film Center outfitted with a handful of ruby banquettes and vases of wildflowers. The day embarks with fresh pastries, such as ollalieberry muffins, and assorted egg dishes and moves on to chicken and grape salad wrapped in toasted almond crepes, steak salad with grilled onions and blue cheese and sandwiches such as king salmon with baby fennel. Everything is available to take away, including boxed lunches tailor-made for a ramble in the nearby woods or seashore.

BESPOKE BAGS AND SHOES
22 April in Paris
Suzanne George Shoemaker
55 Clement Street

For Beatrice Amblard, who apprenticed and designed for Hermès, the smell of leather, glue and wax is more intoxicating than perfume. The only Hermès designer to open a boutique stateside, Amblard crafts custom handbags, accessories – even car interiors – from all manner of skins (calf, ostrich, alligator), saddlestitches them in 200-year-old tradition, and leaves her logo in the form of an 18-karat gold or silver bee (an allusion to her name). For those don't have time to wait, samples can be bought on the spot. The sample shoes in the showroom are by Suzanne George, who fled the financial world to follow her passion to Cordwainers Technical College in London. After various apprenticeships (one with designer Johnny Moke) she came home to produce made-to-measure shoes for fashion shows and individual clients. Styles range from orange raw-silk mules with bead fringe, suitable for a monsoon wedding, to polished leather lace-up wingtip pumps with wrapped Florentine wedges and lacing houndstooth fabric day shoes with bulbous court heels – Virginia Woolf meets Twiggy – which all fit and feel like a second skin.

POSTMORTEM JEWEL BOX
23 Columbarium
1 Loraine Court

As final resting places go, this neo-classical, copper-domed rotunda with stained-glass windows, mosaic ceiling, inlaid marble floors and 6,000 elaborately decorated cremation urns (housing the remains of many of the city's founding families) isn't too shabby. Once surrounded by a cemetery, it now sits within a small garden and has tiered circular balconies that share an acoustical curiosity with St Paul's Cathedral – one may carry on a whispered conversation from across the room. Urns vary from the staid to the flamboyant, much like the city itself.

ARTISANAL PIZZAS
24 Pizzetta 211

INVENTIVE SUSHI
25 Kabuto A & S
5121 Geary Boulevard

While the Japan Center is a warren of good sushi bars and noodle houses, when chefs get a night off many head straight for tiny Kabuto, where Sachio Kojima wields the knife and oversees every exquisitely fresh morsel that is served, including playful inventions such as foie gras sushi laced with a berry-balsamic reduction, less common varieties such as bluefin tuna sashimi, and interesting little dishes to round out a meal, such as sake-marinated grilled black cod. The sakes are rated by dryness, greatly improving upon the usual roulette-wheel approach, and Kabuto serves most nights until 11 pm, which in this part of the Richmond is akin to two in the morning.

CLIFFSIDE MUSEUM
26 California Palace of the Legion of Honor
Lincoln Park, at 34th Avenue & Clement Street

Sitting high on a remote headland known as Land's End that overlooks the Pacific Ocean, this take on the Palais de la Légion d'Honneur in Paris was built in 1916 by architect George Applegarth and bequeathed to the city by philanthropist Alma Spreckels to commemorate California soldiers who died in World War I. The collection of ancient and European art spans some 4,000 years, includes a cast of Rodin's *Thinker*, and also reflects Alma's interest in the dramatic arts: among the dance-related sculpture, drawings and costume and set designs are several concepts for Diaghilev's Ballets Russes by Russian avant-garde artists such as Leon Bakst. Behind the museum are stairs leading to the rugged and breathtaking Coastal Trail, which officially begins by the historic (and now somewhat cheesy) Cliff House, and wends all the way to the Golden Gate Bridge.

Nob Hill
Russian Hill
Cow Hollow
Marina

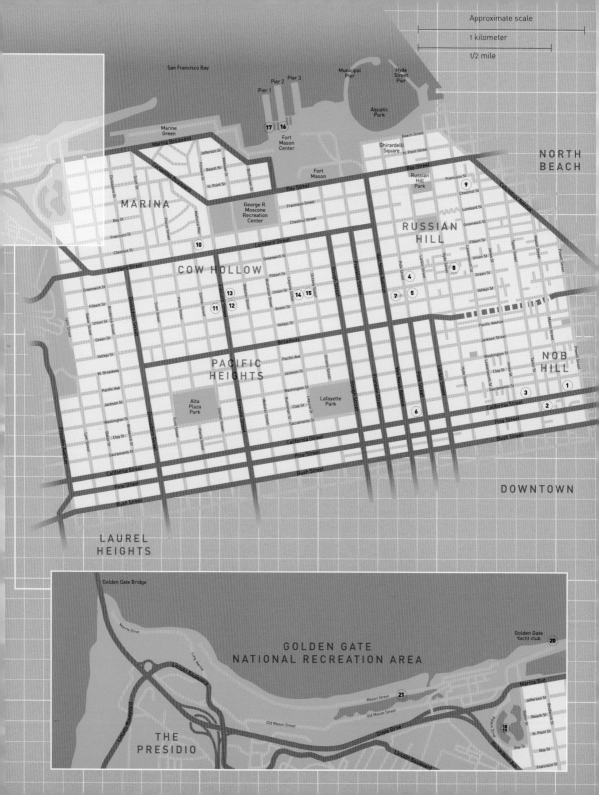

Dubbed the "hill of palaces" by Robert Louis Stevenson, the rarefied eyrie of Nob Hill started attracting the well-heeled in the 1870s, after the invention of cable cars provided a connection to downtown. The claque of railroad tycoons and robber barons known as the "Big Four" set up housekeeping here, and live on in the place names — Huntington, Crocker, Stanford, Hopkins — scattered about the hill and beyond, although their castles were cremated in the fires after the Great Quake. Among the exclusive hotels located here, the vine-covered Huntington (page 114) is the most discreetly posh.

While it's mused that Nob Hill derived its name from the resident "nabobs," Russian Hill memorializes a group of Siberian fur trappers who came through in the early 1800s and are thought to be buried here. Quiet and leafy, the area has a feeling of an urban village, with little restaurants and bars dotting pristine residential streets. The quarter is also a choice destination for an aimless stroll, traced with vertical pedestrian passages such as the Vallejo Street Stairway, designed by architect Willis Polk. Flanked by cottage gardens, the steps embark at Taylor Street by Ina Coolbrith Park and head up to what used to be a warren of artists, writers and architects in the days before real estate became the city's most precious commodity. After the ascent, reward awaits down on Polk Street between Vallejo and Greenwich, newly thick with shops selling antiques, funky collectibles and furniture and a couple of beguiling cafés.

Closer to the water (and just down the hill from Pacific Heights), is Cow Hollow, a former dairy pasture now trodden by ruminating shoppers, especially along Union Street. From here, one should skip Chestnut (a singularly bland high street) and head for the few miles of Marina waterfront between Fort Mason (page 94) and Fort Point, the brick citadel from which Kim Novak threatened to leap into the churning froth in *Vertigo*. You'll pass Bernard Maybeck's Palace of Fine Arts and lagoon (page 94) — all that remains of the fanciful structures created for the 1915 Panama–Pacific Exposition — and through Crissy Field, a former airfield restored to marshland and coastal dunes, with wooden promenades, piers and picnic tables. A trail by the Warming Hut leads to the Golden Gate Bridge. To traverse it by foot — walking at times literally through the clouds as the traffic thrums beneath your feet — is a primal experience that cannot be duplicated by car. Instead of the more typical grey, its swooping spans are painted International Orange, a warm vermilion that makes a lovely foil to the city on one side, to the blue and grey of the sky and water, and to the grasses of the Marin headlands — either green or golden, depending upon the season.

GOTHIC GRANDEUR
3 Grace Cathedral
1100 California Street

This Episcopalian place of worship sits on the site of a robber baron's former mansion (not adverse to earthly rewards, Charles Crocker once owned most of the block). Although its style is distinctly old Europe, the pseudo-Gothic structure is made of earthquake-safe poured concrete. And while quick by Gaudí standards, this cathedral took some time getting built – work began in 1927 and wrapped up in the mid-1960s. Among the appointments are a façade designed after Notre Dame, gilded bronze doors cast from molds of Lorenzo Ghiberti's "Gates of Paradise" in Florence's Baptistery, a rose window made in Chartres, English Carillon bells and a prayer labyrinth for barefoot pilgrims designed after the Chartres original. Among the modern touches are an AIDS Interfaith Chapel with altarpiece by Keith Haring and windows that celebrate secular heroes such as Albert Einstein.

C'EST SI BON
4 Boulange de Polk
2310 Polk Street

Like Pascal Rigo's other bakeries, Boulange de Polk is authentically artisanal, and feels at home in this newly refurbished (and frankly francophilic) quarter of home and garden shops, antique stores and restaurants (his Petit Robert is a few doors away). The rustic breads are baked with organic flour and have a toothsome crust, and the pastries (caramel cannelés, goat-cheese and fig tart, chocolate chip madeleines) mingle French tradition with local ingredients. At breakfast and lunch (baguette sandwiches, toasted tartines, salads) people jockey for space at the communal indoor table and sidewalk seating.

MAGPIE DESIGNER
5 Swallowtail
2217 Polk Street

Interior designer Sheri Sheridan isn't a snob about provenance – she's as happy to display big old red-and-white

enameled gas station numbers as 19th-century art pottery, a 1920s coffin-caddy-cum-coffee-table, hand-painted bust of Dante's Beatrice and a guild-era carpenter's sign. The rococo holds court next to the current and somehow it all tells a cohesive story. Across town, Sheridan's new venture, Noon (page 50), is uniting more than a dozen like-minded designer magpies under one roof.

ATTIC TREASURES
7 Prize
1415 Green Street

From the pink-and-red striped awning outside, to the collection of loving-cup trophies for swim meets, tennis matches and diving contests long past, Prize is a prettified trip down collective memory lane. Old metal apothecary cabinets are filled with antique Steiff animals and puppets, which are joined by vintage glass cake pedestals, pillows embroidered with the states of the Union, and funny children's toys, puzzles and books – all of which evoke a kind of warm and fuzzy nostalgia for an era before video games, George W. and global warming.

GROOVE FACTOR
8 Bacchus Wine and Sake Bar
1954 Hyde Street
Sushi Groove
1916 Hyde Street

When nightlife and music promoters Martel and Nabiel opened their first Sushi Groove, they spotted an empty room a few doors down the street, noted that it faced Jack Kerouac's former house, and deemed it to have lounge potential. With eight barstools, some leather loveseats and a DJ, this intimate bar/art gallery is its own little chill space, where sake cocktails, about fifty wines from small producers (including Lebanon) and sexy downtempo and deep house music create a laid-back Bacchanalia. You can come back the next morning from seven till noon for coffee and pastries baked by a veteran of Citizen Cake. Bacchus is also a fine place to nurse a sake Martini while waiting for a table at Sushi Groove, which makes up in creativity what it lacks in a kitchen. More laid-back than its sister restaurant across town, the blond wood bar serves up inspired combinations, such as a monkey roll (uni, unagi and avocado), tuna tartare salad and a seaweed salad sparked with chili flakes.

Hidden up a steep slope in Russian Hill, the Art Institute building was designed along the lines of a colonial mission, with a pretty courtyard and fountain, cloisters, bell tower and red tiled roof. Even if you're not enrolled in its prestigious program, you can buy painting supplies and postcards in its store and enjoy sweeping views of the bay from the café. The other draw is Diego Rivera's mural, *The Making of a Fresco Showing the Building of a City*, which depicts a large wooden scaffold that frames seminal scenes in San Francisco's construction. Rivera also makes an appearance, his back to the viewer.

Isa sits in dignified anonymity on a packed corridor of the Marina district. Slip through velvet curtains to enter a sleek industrial California–French bistro, tiny on the inside but expanded by a magical tented patio illuminated by candlelight. Chef Luke Sung (who lives upstairs with his family) prepares a shifting repertoire of small plates based on season and whim. Specials such as seared foie gras with sautéed nectarines, veal sweetbreads with mushrooms and halibut drizzled with olive tapenade keep regulars returning. Dishes are all served family-style, so work it out with your companions lest a small riot break out over the last lavender-crusted lamb chop.

Awash with color, texture and a kind of refined eccentricity, Workshop is a fish out of water in its Cow Hollow neighborhood (endowed with not one but two GAP stores). The designs are artful (and expensive) rather than blandly sexy – think Bohemian with a platinum card. It's worth the trek for shimmery, Arabian Nights separates by Dosa (Angelino Christina Kim's elusive line), Matta's city sarongs and ethnic-inspired tops, shoes and scarves, Ann-Louise Roswald's opera coats hand-printed with upholstery florals and Emma Hope's fantastical footwear. But wait, there's more! A cottage in the back garden is entirely turned over to lingerie and swimsuits with a similarly ethereal ethos.

The Luddites of the skincare world, Deborah Burnes and Kila Peterson cook up their skin-beautifying products by hand and in small batches – no machines, chemicals or other labor-saving devices. They call themselves "body chefs," which sounds a tad odd until you smell and smear on the herb-, flower- and fruit-enhanced concoctions, many of which seem to have a culinary bent: butter-enriched bath fizzers in coconut and orange cream that animate the water sans Jacuzzi; chocolate-orange and fruity sorbet salt scrubs that polish the skin to a high glow, and any number of avocado-, goat-milk- and honey-enhanced creams, oils and masques.

Designer and Virginia native Ken Wingard considers his shop of pretty paraphernalia for the home to be "a little a mod, a little old-fashioned: somewhere between an ice-cream shop and a love lounge." The colors of his ceramics, leather goods, lamps, pillows and mobiles ("Mo-bi-le-os") vibrate in tones such as Ice Pop Blue, Sprout Green and High Heel Red, each delicious in its own way and tempered by the essential, streamlined shapes that reflect Wingard's background as a Princeton-trained architect.

This quaint, cozy trattoria is an oasis of civility on a block of sports-bar-studded Union Street. Keith Luce oversees the kitchen, which turns out rich northern Italian dishes (with ingredients and techniques by way of France and California), while his wife, Raney, oversees the intimate dining room and wine bar accented by rich, bordello-red walls. Their novel formula allows you to compile a two-, three-, or four-course meal from the entire menu, which might translate into two main courses – roasted free-range chicken with organic beets and aged balsamico and house-made pappardelle with duck confit – or two appetizers, say, capped with a warm chocolate *budino*.

16 Fort Mason Center

- African American Historical & Cultural Society, Building C
- Museo ItaloAmericano, Building C
- Museum of Craft & Folk Art, Building A
- Mexican Museum, Building D

The Golden Gate National Recreation Area, which stretches from shore to shore and is more than twice as large as the city proper, is headquartered at Fort Mason, a former dockside military base that now houses myriad non-profit and cultural institutions. The African American Historical & Cultural Society operates a museum, gallery and gift shop, as does the Museo ItaloAmericano. At the Museum of Craft & Folk Art, works range from tattooing to Japanese fabric dyeing. The Mexican Museum, whose 12,000 objects spanning thousands of years of Mexican history forms the stuff of varied exhibitions, will soon be moving to expanded digs near Yerba Buena Center.

VEGETARIAN ICON

17 Greens Restaurant
Fort Mason Center, Building A

When Greens was founded by the Zen Center in 1979, vegetarian fare was defined by gummy brown rice and steamed veggies. Greens changed all that, with soulful, inventive and expertly prepared food that has always been equally attractive to omnivores (as are the sweeping views of the bay). Chef Annie Somerville serves housemade pasta with chanterelles, spicy yellow lentil curry and vegetable-ricotta-Gruyère pancakes in tomato-sherry sauce in a room with high ceilings and appointed with twelve types of wood – from redwood tabletops to massive black walnut doors.

MAYBECK'S MONUMENT

18 Palace of Fine Arts
3301 Lyon Street

Bay Area architect Bernard Maybeck's contribution to the grand Panama–Pacific International Exposition of 1915 was a dreamy mock-Roman ruin built on the edge of a swan-filled lagoon. The Corinthian columns, octagonal arcade topped with a domed rotunda and friezes of weeping women create a spot both sylvan and melancholy – ideal for a picnic. Like all of the structures built for the Expo, the Palace was meant to stand for only a year, but as the city didn't have the heart to demolish it they left it to crumble slowly instead. Starting in 1964, workers carefully removed the original design elements from which molds were made and replaced the rotunda and colonnade with concrete casings, leaving a faithful, stripped-down version of Maybeck's original.

TOUCHING ENCOURAGED

19 Exploratorium
Palace of Fine Arts, 3601 Lyon Street

At this interactive museum of science, art and human perception, visitors learn everything from the mysteries of DNA and the way the human eye works to the science behind skateboarding and tornadoes. Far from a dull tour, the Exploratorium encourages viewers to touch, manipulate and experience its 650 exhibits and experiments. Most notable is the Tactile Dome, which invites you to crawl, climb and slide through a maze of different textures in complete darkness, using only your sense of touch as guide (advance reservation required).

UNDERWATER SYMPHONY

20 Wave Organ
Marina Green, Yacht Road

It's a short stroll from the Palace of Fine Arts to this jutting spit of land. Part art installation, part underwater musical instrument, periscope-like pipes protrude through the jetty's carved granite and marble blocks and benches made from the remains of a dismantled Gold Rush-era cemetery. Like some lost room of Atlantis, the Wave Organ channels the ebbing and flowing of the bay's currents into an eerie kind of music more akin to muffled gurgles and sighs than a Bach Cantata.

SEASIDE STROLL

21 Crissy Field
Between the Palace of Fine Arts and Fort Point

Not so long ago, these hundred acres of meadows, tidal marshes, dunes, beaches, wooden promenades and native plant habitats were a strip of asphalt surrounded by a chainlink fence. Now that the former military airfield has been restored to its previous glory, Crissy Field is attracting wildlife not seen in more than half a century – along with strollers, joggers, cyclists, sunbathers and the usual loons who turn out when this often mist-shrouded area turns sunny. Toward the fishing end of Crissy Field, at the base of the Golden Gate Bridge, the glass Warming Hut offers shelter and simple, delicious snacks that have been vetted by Alice Waters, such as grilled sandwiches, clam chowder, hot cocoa and organic espresso.

Berkeley
Oakland

To drive fifteen minutes over the Bay Bridge or take a BART train under the water to Berkeley or Oakland is to discover a generally more temperate world, with much to explore — from the woodsy campus of the University of California at Berkeley, established at its current site in 1873, to the sprawling monthly flea market in Alameda (page 104), which draws dealers from around the world. To make sense of the many miles in between, we've focused on clustered attractions with scattered highlights — and added a few more below to help orient the traveler with more time to wander.

Berkeley and revolution are synonymous, whether it's the Free Speech Movement, born during the peak of the Vietnam War protests, or the culinary overhaul cooked up in the Arts and Crafts–style building that houses Chez Panisse (page 138). A visit to the campus area might include a trip up the Campanile, with its 61-bell carillon and panoramic views, and a stroll to the often provocative Berkeley Art Museum (founded with seed money provided by abstract expressionist Hans Hofmann) and Pacific Film Archive, a kind of left-coast Cinémateque Française, whose rotating repertory embraces everything from Blaxploitation to Red Hollywood and retrospectives from Sirk to Chabrol. Among the cheek-by-jowl shops on Fourth Street by the Berkeley marina are a clutch of genuinely intriguing and independent boutiques, bookstores and restaurants that more than warrant the trip (page 100). And head-clearing nature can be found at the Berkeley Rose Garden and up in the hills, at Tilden Park's 2,000 acres of hiking and biking trails, carrousel and campgrounds.

With a single aphorism, "There is no there there," Gertrude Stein famously dismissed her girlhood home of Oakland, which has become a refuge for increasing numbers of city folk exiled by spiraling housing costs but loath to leave the area. In fact, there is plenty of here here — though not all neighborhoods are entirely safe. College Avenue connects South Berkeley to North Oakland in Rockridge, along blocks of wood-shingled houses, quirky shops, vintage bookstores and destination restaurants such as Oliveto (page 139). Oakland's thriving Chinatown (bounded by 7th, 11th, Broadway and Harrison) is the country's fifth largest, with restaurants (such as Peony) more geared to residents than tourists. The Friday Farmers' Market (9th and Broadway) is a good place to embark on a stroll through Old Oakland, a Victorian enclave whose grand brick hotels, now at the heart of the urban revival, were built to accommodate travelers on the old Transcontinental Railroad. Caffe 817 (page 104) and Le Cheval (a Vietnamese favorite of locals and politicos) represent the culinary diversity that abounds in today's Oakland.

1 Vik's Chaat Corner

724 Allston Way

Precious little attention was paid to the interior design of Vik's, a warehouse-like space next to an Indian import company. Instead, it feels more like a bustling New Delhi bazaar, and that's fine with the throngs of expectant diners waiting to choose from the list of absurdly cheap, impeccably fresh chaat served in paper cartons. Mango lassi is the beverage of choice to accompany the many savory filled and flat puri, curries and other spicy treats.

2 Erica Tanov

1827 Fourth Street

Designer Erica Tanov first set up shop in the Berkeley building where her grandfather ran his laundry business, before moving to this airy, high-ceilinged space and branching out to NoLIta in New York. Women cross the bridge for Tanov's trademark feminine-but-not-fussy trousers and jackets, floaty slip skirts and dresses, and paper-thin Indian wallpaper-print cotton pieces in luscious colors, which are displayed on antique tables and cabinets along with her dreamy bedlinens and cashmere sweaters by Mathilde. In the back nook, whimsical, scaled-down separates for infants and children are joined by handknit caps and hand-picked vintage wear.

3 O Chamé

1830 Fourth Street

In a space handcrafted to evoke the calm of a Japanese country teahouse, David Vardy serves a fusion menu that lists now East, now West. Vardy spent years studying tai chi with a Taoist master before following his culinary inclinations, first baking tea cakes of such quality that teahouses in Japan imported them. A meal might start with plates of seared tuna sashimi or grilled eel with endive, then proceed to ceramic bowls of udon noodles topped with smoked trout or pristine plates of grilled skirt steak with mushrooms and artichokes. At lunch, bento boxes may be enjoyed in the front garden, with a cup of tea or cold sake from the voluminous selection.

4 Fourth Street

- The Gardener, no. 1836
- Zinc Details, no. 1842
- Hear Music, no. 1809B
- Bette's Oceanview Diner, no. 1807
- Tacubaya. no. 1788

Some years back, the once-industrial, three-block stretch of Fourth Street by the Berkeley marina was colonized with one restaurant and a few retail outlets. Today, some grumble that it has evolved into an outdoor shopping mall, albeit one with a clutch of enticing boutiques (including a few devoted to children's toys and clothing). At The Gardener, Alta Tingle offers wares for latter-day Gertrude Jekylls as well as armchair horticulturalists, who float in for handblown vessels, Japanese flower-arranging tools, glossy books on Marjorelle and earthenware bowls for mounding onions and peaches. Zinc Details' Vasilio Kiniris is a friendly modernist, whose dedication to contemporary design doesn't eschew comfort or ecstatic bursts of color. Clean without being sterile, his gathering of Japanese and European designs dovetails with the house line of dinnerware, lighting and accessories. (The sister store at 1905 Fillmore Street has an adjacent furniture showroom.) Poke your head into Hear Music and you'll see people wearing headphones, gazing thoughtfully, heads bobbing. Listening hubs are constructed around ever-changing themes – all-night road trips, post-breakup wallowing, surfing – as well as interviews with artists (in which we learn that Tom Waits would pick the Pogues for a drive across Texas). Selections transcend genres and decades – from Johnny Cash to Johnny Rotten, Morphine to Codeine, Beck to Brel to Bally Sagoo. Named after the neighborhood in Mexico City where architect Louis Barragon makes his home, the taqueria Tacubaya is from the proprietors of Doña Tomas (page 104), who take Mexican cooking as seriously as its architecture. Authentic and mostly organic dishes include eggs revueltos – scrambled with chilis, tomatoes and sweet cactus paddles – and frijoles con todos, a rich broth of sliced avocado, pinto beans and Oaxacan cheese. Over at Bette's the décor and bottomless coffee cups are old-school diner, but the ubiquitous line is for such latterday dishes as soufflé-style banana rum pancakes, a BLT with thick-cut pepper bacon, grilled polenta and farm-fresh eggs-over-easy. (It's the greasy spoon minus most of the grease.)

ROSARIAN'S CATHEDRAL
7 Berkeley Rose Garden
Euclid Avenue & Bayview Place

Thousands of rose bushes fill this garden, nestled into a dramatic ravine in the North Berkeley Hills. One of the first Civil Works Projects under the WPA, the garden sits on a park with adjacent tennis courts, hiking trails and foot bridges, and offers a prime vantage point for watching the sun sink behind the Golden Gates. The garden's massive, 220-foot redwood pergola covered in climbing roses and terraced stone amphitheater were suggested by architect Bernard Maybeck, who created the Palace of Fine Arts across the bay.

VIVA LA REVOLUTION!
8 Cheese Board Collective
1504 Shattuck Avenue

Back in the 1960s, a lot of earnest folk who talked the talk ended up going bust or reverting to traditional business models. Not this venerable cheese shop and bakery, which sits across the street from Chez Panisse in the heart of Berkeley's gourmet ghetto and is still run along strictly egalitarian lines (and closes for May Day). House-baked pastries and coffee are available weekdays until 10 am, when the cheese and bread side of things takes over (corn onion cheddar, coriander wheat, provolone olive, to name a few). The staff is not only willing but insistent that you sample the St Agur, Istara, Cabot Cheddar, Chevrot or whatever strikes your fancy. The Pizza Collective next door has a cult following for its thin-crusted vegetarian slices – with toppings like mozzarella, corn, zucchini, onion, feta and cilantro served with a wedge of lime.

SWEET LICKS
12 Mondo Gelato
2106 Shattuck Avenue

When Maurizio Grande arrived in the new country, he missed the old-style *gelato* he was weaned on – more flavor and less air and fat than American ice cream. He tracked down Salvatore Russo, a master gelato maker in Rome (who apprenticed in the mystical ice-cream making arts as a Sicilian teenager), and commissioned him to design Mondo's ever-expanding list of flavors. Gelati include pistachio, malted and rose; *sorbetti* are seasonally inspired – from black mission fig to pear and rhubarb.

PRINTED MATTER
13 Moe's Books
2476 Telegraph Avenue

Moe's isn't quite the same since Moe Moskowitz passed on in 1997. One misses him, stogy in hand, gleefully defying the city's anti-smoking ordinance, surrounded by books he was buying, selling and throwing into heaps while holding forth on any number of topics. But his spirit lives on among these four floors of used, new and antiquarian books, and even in a city known for its bookstores, there's something endearing about this shop that shares its founder's generalist passions for subjects too numerous to contain in neat stacks.

CHURCH OF MAYBECK
14 Church of Christ Scientist
2619 Dwight Way

Many consider this 1910 church sitting behind a high-gabled, wisteria-smothered portico to be visionary architect Bernard Maybeck's masterpiece, although he's better known for the Palace of Fine Arts (page 94) that followed a few years later. The only building in Berkeley to have been declared a National Landmark, the edifice was built with common materials – exposed concrete, industrial sash windows, redwood trellises – and seamlessly integrates Gothic tracery and allusions to Byzantine, Romanesque and Japanese styles into its Craftsman vernacular. Writes Maybeck historian Kenneth H. Cardwell: "No other building demonstrates so completely Maybeck's imaginative architectural genius…with its masterly handling of space, structure, color and light."

SECRET GARDEN

15 Citron/À Côté

131

OTHERWORLDLY TREASURES

16 Tail of the Yak

2632 Ashby Avenue

To walk into this enchanted land of bric-a-brac is like stepping into a fairy tale. Lauren Swan McIntosh and Alice Hoffman Erb curate a kind of bazaar where 19th-century Santos figures sit amidst embroidered Indian shawls, rococo ribbons, richly printed paper goods by Swan Papel, antique jewelry and artist Anandamayi Arnold's mini piñatas – black crows for Halloween, glittery lumps of coal at Christmas. As McIntosh is a teacher of calligraphy, there's always a good selection of pens and inks.

A CHEF'S CHEF

17 Oliveto Restaurant and Café

139

CASTLE IN THE AIR

18 Claremont Resort and Spa

126

EXQUISITE EPHEMERA

19 Addison Endpapers

169

CONVIVIAL COCINA

20 Doña Tomas

5004 Telegraph Avenue

With scarlet walls, high ceilings, low lighting, Mission-style furniture and Mexican artwork adorning the white-washed walls, Doña Tomas transports diners from Oakland to somewhere closer to Oaxaca. Sipping a house margarita and consuming fresh hand-mashed guacamole or just-roasted pumpkin seeds is a warm-up for the fresh, mostly organic dishes that follow, such as gazpacho of heirloom tomatoes, a lime-kissed scallop ceviche, carnitas with free-range Niman Ranch pork and crispy crab tostadas.

DÉCO PALACE

21 Paramount Theatre of the Arts

2025 Broadway

The most dazzling of the extant Art Déco movie palaces, the Paramount, was built in 1931 by architect Timothy L. Pflueger and decorated with a monumental façade mosaic, a towering amber Fountain of Light at the lobby entrance and painted lifesize statues of Egyptian maidens. Although tours are available, the best way to explore the theatre is to enjoy a cocktail in the bar and see a film revival – everything from Abel Gance's *Napoleon* to *The Good, the Bad and the Ugly.*

SIMPLE PLEASURES

22 Caffe 817

817 Washington Street

Alessandro Rossi, Florentine by birth and electrical engineer by trade, spotted an old butcher's shop in a restored swathe of downtown called "Old Oakland" and envisioned an artful hangout. A league of craftspeople created creamy walls, a sinuous concrete-and-mahogany counter and exposed beams that serve as backdrop to Rossi's simple but elegant menu. The star at breakfast is polenta served either with poached eggs and taleggio or an inspired swirl of maple syrup. Lunch brings beautiful little sandwiches, such as the PLT (pancetta, lettuce and tomato), rice-and-borlotti-bean soup, pizzas and daily pastas.

INSIDER ART GALLERY

23 Creative Growth Art Center

355 24th Street

Before the terms "Outsider Art" or "l'Art Brut" had much currency, Creative Growth founded the first visual arts program and gallery for severely disabled adults. Shown in themed exhibitions ("Home," "Fantastic Journey") are collectible hooked rugs, paintings, wood sculptures and ceramics, with proceeds going to the artists. The studio also places works in private collections, galleries and museums throughout the world (Palais Joyce in Paris, Shisedo Foundation in Tokyo, the American Museum of Folk Art in New York), and some of the artists have attained solo status, such as Judith Scott, whose mixed-media work has been compared to that of Louise Bourgeois.

BURIED TREASURE

24 Alameda Point Antiques Market

Alameda Point Naval Station

This huge outdoor flea market adjacent to a National Wildlife Refuge is the anti-eBay, where more than 800 dealers gather on the first Sunday of the month to show their wares. Because everything sold must be at least twenty years old and no reproductions are allowed, there are no piles of tube socks and "authentic" Déco recreations, and the market has become a magnet for global collectors.

sleep

In this diminutive city of distinctive neighborhoods, where you choose to lay your head depends upon which version of San Francisco you wish to inhabit. If it's the Beat Bohemianism of North Beach, then head for tiny, color-washed Hotel Bohème. For Victorian grandeur, hotels such as the historic Archbishop's Mansion and Majestic effectively channel that clawfoot-tub-and-crystal-chandelier past. Looking for theatrical modernity and a built-in nightlife? Check into Clift — the only über-design hostelry in the city — or the groovy Phoenix, a few blocks on. And so it goes, from the water's edge (Hotel Griffon), to the Huntington at the crest of Nob Hill — a San Francisco to suit all types.

STARCK REALITY

14 **Clift**

15 495 Geary Street

Rooms from $250

By turns gorgeous, amusing, silly, luxurious and lush, Clift is the kind of high-design, high-concept lodging that the city lacked until Ian Schrager and Philippe Starck catapulted this 1913 Italianate structure into the 21st century.

It makes sense that Clift is in the theater district, considering that Schrager and Starck sought a dreamy and surrealist "down the rabbit hole" esthetic. It's a little bit Brothers Quay, a little bit rock and roll. The hotel's monumental proportions encouraged playing with scale, and Starck obliged with a Brobdingnagian lobby chair upholstered in antique tapestry, reception desk hand-wrought from a single piece of solid mahogany and an 18-foot (5.5-meter) carved bronze mantel by Gerard Garouste that rises above the eternally lit fire. Some design asides are in the nudge-and-a-wink category – a Magritte-alluding black bowler with green apple stool and the egg-topped table by Salvador Dalí. Classic pieces, such as the Jean Nouvel metal concierge desk, pull everything together. The lounge area off the lobby is a sort of tweaked drawing room, where photographic portraits of plastic toy animals (taken by Jean Baptiste Mondino) gaze out in place of family portraits. But it's with the redesign of the venerable old Art Déco Redwood Room bar (page 152) that tradition and modernity meet head on and survive to tell the tale.

Soothing in shades of gray and lavender, the 375 roomy guestrooms (which include lofts, studios and suites) are furnished with massive English sycamore sleigh beds – and 400-thread-count sheets and down duvet to go with them – a complete entertainment center and Man Ray-inspired wooden chairs with wheels. Two large mirrors encourage navel (and other parts) gazing. And day-glo orange acrylic night tables were reportedly inspired by the hue of the sun setting over the Pacific.

74 **Hotel Majestic**

2 1500 Sutter Street
Rooms from $220

Constructed in 1902 as the private residence of railroad magnate Milton Schmidt, this five-story, 58-room Edwardian in Pacific Heights was converted to the Hotel Majestic when the peripatetic Mr. Schmidt moved on two years later. Spared the devastating fires of the 1906 'quake, it's the city's oldest continuously operating hotel.

When designer Candra Scott was approached to thoroughly renovate the building in 1985, she pored over original photographs, then headed for Europe and hit the antiques markets. Back came 18th-century Chinese screens, Austrian Biedermeier chairs, French Empire chandeliers and the granite-topped, horseshoe-shaped mahogany bar that once held court in a Paris bistro and now dispenses drinks in the hotel's clubby Avalon Bar (which also houses an elaborate butterfly collection filled with rare specimens from Africa and New Guinea). Layered with tapestries, tasseled brocades, tchokes with provenance and down-filled sofas, the lobby retains the feeling of a private Edwardian residence – and the "more-is-more" theme extends to the suites (which have gas-burning fireplaces and stellar views) and guestrooms, many of which have clawfoot tubs. Complimentary breakfast is served in the hotel's Perlot restaurant.

In addition to its creature comforts (Turkish robes, feather pillows, turndown service), Hotel Majestic is nicely tucked away from the madding crowd yet within close striking distance of many neighborhoods. Turn one way for the quirky shops and restaurants of Hayes Valley and the Beaux Arts grandeur of the Asian Art Museum, Opera House and City Hall in Civic Center; head the other to stroll up to Pacific Heights, with its sprawling parks, boutique-studded streets and even tonier opportunities for spending money.

NOB HILL HIDEAWAY

88 **Huntington Hotel**

2 1075 California Street
Rooms from $320

Hills attract wealth, and Nob Hill, being the city center's highest peak, has tended to attract the biggest 'nobs.' Back in the days of the Wild West, the great railroad barons came here to put down stakes – among them C. P. Huntington, whose mansion sat on the park across from the Huntington Hotel. Today, this ivy-smothered, family-owned landmark is as famous for its discretion and service (the staff-to-guest ratio is one to one) as for its A-list guest list.

The twelve-story hotel – the first brick-and-steel highrise west of the Mississippi – was built in 1924 to house luxury apartments. In 1945, when the building was converted to a tourist hotel, the apartments were not reduced in size nor redesigned for conformity. Anthony Hail is perhaps the most notable of the society designers to have left his mark on the 100 roomy guestrooms and 35 suites in the form of rich fabrics, antiques and artwork. You can walk out the front door and hop on a cable car or stroll the short distance to Union Square, Chinatown or North Beach.

Because life at the top can be stressful, it's no small incentive that the Huntington offers guests use of its Nob Hill Spa, a light-infused, three-story pleasure dome with indoor infinity pool, steam rooms, fireside lounge and 18-foot (5.5-meter) windows looking out to the city.

60 Hotel Griffon

 155 Steuart Street
Rooms from $180

When the Hotel Griffon went up in 1906, nobody imagined that its bay-facing windows would one day stare out at a freeway – and only a seer could have predicted that, decades later, an earthquake would restore the view. In fact, guests of this hotel are among the prime beneficiaries of nature's 1989 temper tantrum.

Set along a pretty, tree-lined block of restaurants on the Embarcadero, Hotel Griffon is what is often described as "European," which is to say charming and comfortable without being ostentatious. Many of the 62 rooms have their original whitewashed brick walls and the décor is clean and uncluttered, with high ceilings, mahogany writing desks and window seats. The top floor has been given over to suites, some with private furnished terraces, others with vistas of the water. Breakfast is complimentary and room service is available from the seafood-centric Red Herring Restaurant and Bait Bar, located just off the lobby.

An easy walk to downtown the Griffon is a scant block from the refurbished Ferry Building (page 164). Glance in the other direction and you'll see Claes Oldenburg and Coosje van Bruggen's 60-foot (18-meter) sculpture, *Cupid's Span*, planted on the grassy slopes of Rincon Park. From certain angles, it appears as if an arrow is being shot right into the bay.

14 **Phoenix Hotel**

18 601 Eddy Street
Rooms from $130

The Phoenix has been associated with a landmark nightspot since opening over a decade ago. Recently, from the ashes of Backflip rose the Bambuddha Lounge, which is striving for that Hotel Costes vibe with a pedigreed house DJ and guest spinners (such as Gotan Project). This is a hotel that knows how to party and has always been a destination for people in the entertainment industry (and those who aspire to be). Which is a long way of saying that if sleep is your top priority, this may not be your first choice of hostelry.

The original 1950s architecture has been kept largely intact, as has the outdoor heated swimming pool around which much of the action swirls. All 44 rooms and suites are furnished in tropical island bungalow idiom, and continental breakfast is served poolside to those able to face the morning light. Once you do get moving, the quasi-edgy Tenderloin locale is within easy striking distance of Downtown, Civic Center and Hayes Valley.

Overseen by a reclining rooftop Buddha, the lounge serves refined pan-Asian cuisine and sweet cocktails amidst waterfalls and a scattering of Asian artifacts. The open space flows into intimate nooks with low-slung tables and leather daybeds and continues into the heated poolside bar, which is encircled by a stand of giant bamboo that sways to the mix of ambient, hip-hop, funk and house.

DELICIOUS VICTORIAN EXCESS

44 **The Archbishop's Mansion**

17 1000 Fulton Street

Rooms from $150

Everything about the Archbishop's Mansion is cheerfully over-the-top, as you'd expect from a place where the Bechstein piano formerly owned by Noel Coward is illuminated by a chandelier featured in *Gone with the Wind*. Built in 1904 in French chateau style for the Archbishop of San Francisco (apparently unperturbed by vows of poverty), it has a mahogany staircase sweeping up three floors towards 15 stately guestrooms and a large leaded-glass dome.

The *Upstairs Downstairs* drama begins in bed, when a tricked-out breakfast is brought to your door, and continues at the evening reception in the parlor. With guests gathered around the carved wood fireplace, wine glasses in hand, it's a bit like being on the film set of a murder mystery, waiting for the inspector to arrive.

Perhaps because of the Mansion's grandeur, the ten rooms and five suites are all named for operas (the Don Giovanni Suite being the Archbishop's former digs, ironically enough). Beds are topped with canopies, and many of the rooms have fireplaces and either old-fashioned tubs or whirlpool baths – the Carmen Suite's clawfoot tub sits right before the fire. While there are enough frills and furbelows to fill a regional version of *Antiques Roadshow*, they do not come at the expense of the mod cons (VCR, CD player) that make contemporary life so charming.

Sitting on quiet leafy Alamo Square, the Mansion is just across from the most frequently photographed group of Victorian "Painted Ladies" – the Queen Anne-style houses also known as the "Six Sisters." And while part of the hotel's charm is the residential location, it's but a pleasant stroll down to the shops and cafés of the Hayes Valley or up to Pacific Heights and a short hike to the Haight Ashbury and Golden Gate Park, with its myriad gardens, rowing lake, bison paddock, aquarium and other amusements.

Just a block off the shopping frenzy of Union Square, the clubby lobby and bar of the Hotel Rex recalls an era before megastores. Named for poet Kenneth Rexroth, the leader of the San Francisco Poetry Renaissance who served as a mentor to the beat writers who followed, it's modeled on art and literary salons of the 1920s and 1930s and furnished with big leather chairs, eccentric objects and walls of antiquarian books. Also a favorite haunt of living writers, the Rex is a gathering place for readings and Algonquin-style roundtable discussions fueled by tea and stronger libations.

Designer Candra Scott (who gave the Hotel Bohème its neo-Beat flavor) commissioned more than a dozen artists to create a truly crafted feeling. The goatskin lampshades are all hand-painted, and new works hang beside oil portraits by Bay Area painters of the past. Scott also searched for objects with historical provenance, such as the sculpture from the 1939 World's Fair that perches on the mantel.

The 92 rooms and two suites continue the men's club theme with dark wood, striped carpets, checked bedspreads and hand-thrown ceramic lamps. During a recent renovation, Egyptian linens, down quilts and pillow-top mattresses were added, and a tiny Franco–Latino bistro (Café Andrée, named for Rexroth's wife) bedecked with period artwork, old books and antique globes is now on the premises. Even the upgraded business centers received the treatment: alongside computer stations with high-speed internet access, vintage typewriters bear quotes from local writers – Jack London, Dashiell Hammett, John Steinbeck and Lillian Hellman – who have not lost their voices in a faster-paced world.

You enter the Hotel Bohème off the street, pass through black and gold draperies, and ascend to a landing bathed in soft light. On the walls, Jerry Stoll's historic black-and-white photographs introduce some of the local heroes (Jack Kerouac, Neal Cassady and the like), for North Beach is a place where the free-spirited ghosts of the poets, painters and poseurs who put it on the map still hold court. Sitting in the very heart of the neighborhood, this intimate, 15-room hotel feels like an authentic part of its milieu rather than some stage-set homage to the past.

Rebuilt soon after the 1906 earthquake, the hotel got a serious facelift in the mid-1990s by designer Candra Scott, who evokes a kind of dreamy, almost Parisian languor with burnt-orange walls and violet doors sparked with green and black. The rooms are cozy, in size and by design, with iron-railed queen-sized beds – some with gauze-draped canopies – antique armoires and a motley of checks, florals and stripes. Lampshades are made from the flotsam of old Blue Note Record sleeves and the covers of City Lights poetry books and upturned Chinese parasols diffuse overhead light. The artist's-garret-with-amenities ambience encourages lingering in bed rather than rushing out to engage in commerce. And yes, Allen Ginsberg *did* sleep here.

CASTLE IN THE AIR

98 Claremont Resort and Spa

 41 Tunnel Road
Rooms from $300

Frank Lloyd Wright, the architect of Fallingwater, called the Claremont Resort "one of the few hotels in the world with warmth, character and charm." Nestling high in the Oakland/Berkeley hills like some enchanted Valhalla, it's hard to believe this white, half-timbered castle is only 12 miles (19 km) from downtown San Francisco.

In fact, the Claremont opened in 1915 on 22 verdant acres (9 hectares) to offer stressed-out city folk an escape from the summer fog. There was swimming and tennis by day, Count Basie, Louis Armstrong and Tommy Dorsey at night (the latter, alas, no longer available). The 279 rooms and 16 suites are large, airy and comfortable in a refined country-lodge kind of way, and many have postcard views of the bay and San Francisco skyline, which often appears swathed in clouds. Although it appears to be sitting halfway to heaven, the Claremont is actually a practical base for exploring the East Bay – about five minutes by car to the restaurants and quirky shops of College Avenue in Rockridge, and not much more to destinations such as Tilden Park, Chinatown, the Oakland Museum and the wildlife sanctuary at Lake Merritt. (The UC Berkeley campus is but a mile away.)

But some, despite their good intentions, never quite make it off the grounds. Guests have free access to the heated pools, tennis courts, fitness center, yoga and other classes, and many of the attractions of the spa, whose massive renovation created a serious temple of relaxation that still attracts San Franciscans seeking respite. Water is everywhere, with two flotation tanks, a whirlpool hot tub and myriad soaking-buffing-massaging treatments that take a New Age, multi-culti approach to getting your glow on: "Mayan Temple Journey," "Zen Trilogy Body Wrap," "Aqua Latte Milk Bath & Moisture Treatment," "Tibetan Sound Massage."

eat

San Francisco is not just a restaurant city, but a place in which food is consumed, considered and discussed with Talmudic passion. (This sometimes borders on the maniacal, with menus providing the provenance of every nut and nettle.) Whatever a chef's approach, the undisputed progenitor for what is called "California Cuisine" is Chez Panisse, at this point approaching creation myth status. What is now taken for granted — basing meals around seasonal ingredients — was nothing less than revolutionary back in 1970s America. Along with the old cuisine went the starchy formality that used to define "fine dining," for this is laid-back California, after all.

Chez Spencer Martini
Ketel One + Noilly Prat Dry
with ICE BALL - 9

Champagne Cocktail
Marie Brizzard Pêche + Champ
- 11.

Makers Mark Mint Ju
Whisky + Fresh Mint - 9

Josephine Baker Martin
vodka, rosewater spritz and a
rose petal. 8

DÉLICES DE CALIFORNIE

14 Chez Spencer

46 82 14th Street

After ambling past warehouses and garages down the semi-deserted sidewalk, you find the bistro's name scrawled in graffiti, pass through a tented patio of olive trees lit with fairy lights, and hear jazz spilling out the door. Step inside, and you'll find chef Laurent Katgely (the restaurant is named for his son) working the woodburning stove in an airy dining room crowned with arching wooden beams and skylights and decorated with an assortment of figure paintings and taxidermy. Katgely practices a kind of bilingual cooking, applying techniques honed at multistarred establishments to his adopted state's freshly harvested ingredients and more casual approach. Most dishes are small but intensely flavorful. One night he might drizzle truffle oil into white corn soup, pair grilled lobster with ripe peaches or seared foie gras with apricot tart, or truffle a risotto with four earthy types of mushroom. The five-course tasting menu (with or without individual wine pairings) takes off after the amuse-bouche like a culinary carnival ride.

98 **Citron**

15 5484 College Avenue

À Côté

5478 College Avenue

Chris Rossi's Citron might look like just another smartly designed bistro, but the food zings – with entrées that play fast and loose with the bistro concept – tandoori spiced chicken breast with lentils and nectarine chutney and wild sturgeon stuffed with sweetbreads. At the aptly named À Côté, Rossi hired chef Matt Colagan to have his way with the ubiquitous small-plate concept. The buzzing room and a heated back patio garden with amethyst velvet drapes and amber glass lights create a magical backdrop for maize soup with spicy prawns and mussels cooked with Pernod in the wood oven.

32 **Delfina**

17 3621 18th Street

You're greeted like an old friend from the first visit – as if there weren't twenty people ready to kill for your table and chef Craig Stoll weren't considered a culinary messiah far beyond the doors of his hip, hot Mission restaurant. The food is similarly inviting – straightforward but soulful Italian in which individual ingredients shine and entrées hover below $20. Stoll apprenticed at da Delfina in the hills of Tuscany, where he learned to do everything from making cheese to curing his own Parma prosciutto, and you can feel his handprints on every dish. Squash blossoms stuffed with ricotta are fried to a glassy, greaseless finish; smoky, grilled calamari are arrayed over warm white beans, tagliatelle alla carbonara is spiked with house-cured guanciale and tender short ribs are slowly braised in Chianti. The spare, modern space is just as welcoming, and there's a counter for hopeful walk-ins. A soon-to-be opened adjacent outpost for Stoll's elegant pizzas and simple antipasti have regulars in something of an expectant dither.

If there's a restaurant that sums up San Francisco's love affair with Mediterranean cuisine and informal dining, it's Zuni (the name reflects an early flirtation with the Southwest). After 25 years, this wedge-shaped café with picture windows facing Market Street is still central to the city's culinary life, and along the way, co-owner Judy Rodgers was named best chef in California by the James Beard foundation. Lunch might be pizza from the wood-burning oven and a lemony Caesar salad. Pre-theater cocktails go well with a plate of crispy piccolo frito, which, like everything, can be enjoyed in the bar. At least one leisurely dinner should include Rodgers's trademark roasted chicken with Tuscan bread salad. And in warm weather, a sidewalk table topped with a platter of briny oysters and a glass of Sancerre is about as good as life gets. Zuni's famous hamburger on focaccia is available after ten o'clock, around the time many restaurants are hanging up their closed signs.

"Why can't it be in *my* neighborhood?" is the question often posed by fans of Tamar Peltz and Ria Ramsey's tiny pizzeria serving lunch and dinner on a residential street in the Richmond district. With just four tables, a small counter and some sidewalk seating (with heat lamps to counter the fog), Pizzetta 211 seduces people from miles away to wait, Peroni beer or wine in hand, for its impossibly thin-crusted pizzas topped with organic and mostly locally made ingredients. While tomato, mozzarella and basil are perennial (with or without pepperoni or white anchovies), specials may be topped with clams and pesto; roasted nectarines, crescenza and prosciutto, or rosemary, fiore sardo and pinenuts. One recent summer's night the calzone was stuffed with Belfiore ricotta, Redwood Hill goat cheese and tomato sauce. There's always an organic farm salad and artisan cheese plate to precede or follow the star pies, and simple sweet bites – saffron biscotti with vin santo or a deliciously gritty polenta cake laced with seasonal fruit – to close with an espresso or cup of Moroccan mint tea.

After a dozen years, Universal's marriage of homey but inventive cooking is still blessed (as is the union of its owners, Armando Avalos and chef Leslie Carr-Avalos). A grilled ribeye may be topped with salsa verde and served on a mound of heirloom tomatoes and fava beans in summer, while winter accompaniments might run to French beans and Gorgonzola mashed potatoes. Starters are designed for sharing – cornmeal crusted sardines, chicken livers and figs grilled en brochette, an omnipresent flatbread topped with seasonal ingredients. Located in the heart of an industrial neighborhood in transition, the warm room with sidewalk tables and handcrafted details was transformed by Larissa and Jeff Sand. Recycled gray marble tops the gently curving bar, a congenial place to sit with a glass of wine and bowl of fresh spaghettini with anchovies at night or a cappuccino and mound of French toast with peach-ginger compote for weekend brunch.

Former film student Elizabeth Faulkner burst upon the dessert scene like some *enfant terrible* of sweets – playing with flavors and applying architectural principles to spun sugar (one of her cakes replicated the Bilbao Guggenheim). Since moving from its original location (now occupied by Chez Spencer), Citizen Cake has evolved from a patisserie offering pastries, chocolates, hearth breads, housemade gelato and, yes, a rose-petal crème brûlée, into a chic restaurant that meets most of one's nutritional needs. You could breakfast on cappuccino and frangipani croissants and choose lunch from the menu of inventive salads, small pizzas and sandwiches such as Cuban marinated pork. Dinner, under the auspices of chef de cuisine Jennifer Cox, might include roasted Szechwan peppersalt chicken with bok choy, green-tea-cured cod or a locally raised lamb shank braised in cumin, coriander and cinnamon with crushed lemon potatoes. And the bar is a fine place to light for a restorative hot chocolate, cocktail or glass of wine. Within this pared-down, light-filled space, the only imperative is to save room for dessert.

Tucked discreetly in a Mission district warehouse, Foreign Cinema has a hook beyond its sexy Cal-Med food and warm yet industrial dining room with roaring fire. At night, classic films – from *de rigueur* Fellini and Cocteau to domestic product by folks like the Coen brothers – are projected onto a whitewashed wall in the heated patio, the flickering images and dialogue (delivered via old-fashioned drive-in speakers) providing a moving backdrop to your meal. Speaking of food, executive chefs and Zuni Café alums Gayle Pirie and husband John Clark have thoroughly revamped the cuisine in the seasonal, organic mode of their former kitchen. The changing menu takes its cues from Spain, France and Italy – as in cured sardines with shaved fennel and mozzarella, beef sirloin carpaccio with crispy leeks, lavender-scented pork chop stuffed with quince, fedelini pasta with tomato "confit," and a well-stocked raw bar.

14 **Kyo-Ya**

28 The Palace Hotel, 2 New Montgomery Street

In a city not short on exceptional sushi bars, this elegantly appointed restaurant diverges from the usual cookie-cutter offerings. It goes without saying that the jewel-like sushi and sashimi are impeccably fresh and perfectly prepared, as are less ubiquitous dishes, such as *chawan-mushi* (freshwater eel, ginkgo nut, sea urchin and mochi), *awabi-to-nasu* (abalone with eggplant), and *sake chazuke* (salmon simmered in light rice soup). But many are drawn by chef Kuni Oshikawa's leisurely *kaiseki* dinners, which unfold like a flower over eight courses and change every month. According to ancient tradition, the dishes are not only visually appealing but also carefully balanced to create a harmony of flavors and textures – fried, pickled, raw and grilled. One night's *kaiseki* included deep-fried baby crab, wine-marinated mountain peach, almond-covered shrimp tempura, assorted sashimi, wasabi-marinated beef, mixed mushrooms with mackerel tossed in balsamic, udon noodles topped with red snapper and a simple, refreshing dessert.

EVOLVED OPULENCE

14 **Fleur de Lys**

22 777 Sutter Street

Although Fleur de Lys has been a destination for almost half a century, it resists riding on its reputation thanks to the creativity and ingenuity of chef-owner Hubert Keller, who trained with Paul Bocuse and was once dubbed "rebel with a Cuisinart" by the *New York Times*. Like something out of Balzac, the mirrored red-and-gold dining room is tented in 900 yards (820 meters) of fabric, and a marble fireplace warms an intimate salon. A three-, four- or five-course tasting menu is chosen from a varied *carte* that reflects the California preference for flavor over heft – monkfish rolled in aged Serrano ham with roasted figs and artichoke flan; lamb loin with spiced honey and cumin seed sauce and mint oil; a foie gras duo featuring truffled soup and seared duck "burger" in brioche bun; crispy veal sweetbreads and lemon-kissed asparagus tips accented with cream of Pacific sea urchin roe. There's a vegetarian tasting menu (Peruvian purple potato stuffed with a warm curry shiitake salad, a summer feast of heirloom tomatoes), and, with notice, Keller will even cook up a vegan option.

32 **Luna Park**

6 694 Valencia Street

The look is neo-bordello flea-market chic, with wine-dark walls, a long bar and crystal-dripping chandeliers, while the omnipresent crowd of (mostly) pretty young things downing mojitos adorned with plastic monkeys creates an unrelenting roar. But unlike other trendy eateries, where it's mostly about being seen, Luna Park turns out serious food while not taking itself too seriously (and lunch is several decibels quieter). Joe Jack and A. J. Gilbert's menu roams the globe – from *Pot au Feu* (translated as "Pot on Fire") to goat-cheese fondue, a Hawaiian tuna "poke" with wonton chips and big salads like Cambazola with watercress, pears and hazelnuts. The do-it-yourself s'mores (molten marshmallow, dark chocolate and housemade graham cookies) are an interactive treat.

32 **Blue Plate**

26 3218 Mission Street

Opening Blue Plate was a labor of love for Cory Obenour and Jeff Trenam, who pulled in favors from friends to transform a deserted space in the Mission outskirts at the foothills of Bernal Heights into what feels like a cross between a cool, arty flat and an old-fashioned diner. Old skateboard decks (donated by one of the chef's grandfathers) share space with moody paintings, mix-matched furniture, chandeliers, flowers arranged in old mackerel tins and creaky wood floors. The bartenders double as DJs (requests cheerfully taken) and the menu is homey, organic California, with everything from grilled local squid, figleaf-wrapped halibut, coriander crusted lamb and house-smoked wild sturgeon to a luscious macaroni and drunken Spanish goat cheese and meatloaf like mom never made. The back garden, filled with fragrant Brugmansia trees dripping yellow blooms and festooned with fairy lights, is a transporting place to nurse a glass of Prosecco or can of cold Olympia brew on a warm night or while waiting for a table.

 Chez Panisse Restaurant and Café

1517 Shattuck Avenue

Both the restaurant and founding chef, Alice Waters, are legends, responsible for fomenting the "delicious revolution" that made words like "seasonal," "organic" and "sustainable" part of the culinary lexicon while supporting the cause of small farmers and local purveyors (the anti-Big Mac). And it would take a genealogical chart to trace how many chefs have graduated from the Chez Panisse kitchen to stoves of their own. Named for a character in the Marcel Pagnol film trilogy *Marius*, *Fanny* and *César*, the wood-shingled arts and crafts building in the heart of Berkeley's "gourmet ghetto" opened its doors thirty years ago and still serves one fixed-price menu each night. As unfussy and unpretentious as they are perfect, the meals build in courses and complexity as the week progresses (nicely matching our moods as the weekend approaches). A recent winter Friday started with an aperitif, followed by squid and artichoke salad, a Livorno fish soup with wine and meat broth, Sonoma County Liberty duck with juniper berries and a radicchio and garlic confit with thyme, and blood-orange and caramel millefoglie. The more casual, bustling upstairs café has its own à la carte menu and a woodburning pizza oven.

98 **Oliveto Restaurant and Café**

 5655 College Avenue

The epicenter of the Rockridge restaurant renaissance is Oliveto, where chef–owner Paul Bertolli inspires critics with frissons of ecstasy (the *New York Times* called him "...one of the two greatest working chefs in the United States") and admiration for his hands-on approach – he makes his own pasta, mills his own polenta, cures his meats and even ages the balsamico in-house. A Chez Panisse alum (he co-authored the *Chez Panisse Cookbook* with Alice Waters), Bertolli is equally devoted to the in-season, organic, sustainably raised mantra, which he pairs with an Italian woodfired grill and rotisserie. The results – charcoal-grilled pigeon with bitter greens and pancetta, tagliolini with local sand dabs, spit-roasted stuffed loin of rabbit with young carrots – elucidate individual ingredients in new ways. Bertolli's special events, such as a "Whole Hog" menu (sounds just like what it is), are wildly popular and take place in the pretty, spare upstairs dining room, which is as unfussy as the food. The buzzing street-level corner café keeps longer hours, and has added a short dinner menu of thin-crusted pizzas, baked pastas and antipasti.

60 **Piperade**

11 1015 Battery Street

Named for a traditional Basque concoction of sauteed peppers, onions, tomatoes and garlic topped with a poached egg, Piperade has all the slow-cooked passion of Gerald Hirigoyen's native cuisine tempered with a freshness well suited to the Californian climate. Born in a small town near Biarritz, Hirigoyen summarizes his approach as "West Coast Basque cuisine." The décor is a similar combination of rustic and light, with oak floors, brick walls, art posters and an oversized "sheepherder's table" offering congenial seating to solo diners. The menu is divided into Tipia (small plates) and Handia (big plates). The former might include Crab Txangurro, which is sparked with mango and pepper salsa; chilled mussel-and-bread salad, and a garlic soup rich with rock shrimp, bacon, bread and egg. Among Handia dishes are braised seafood and shellfish stew in red pepper sauce and chicken breast with star anise, preserved lemon and artichokes. That Hirigoyen embarked on his career as a pastry chef is evident in the melting orange-blossom beignets and gâteau Basque.

60 **Da Flora**

23 701 Columbus Avenue

Flora Gaspar was an art student in Venice when she learned to cook from the housewives in her Rialto neighborhood. Tiring of the gallery world, Gaspar opened her candlelit ristorante in a cozy North Beach corner storefront that she considers an extension of her home. The blood-red walls, flickering candles, Venetian flea market décor and creative wine list create the ideal stage set for dinner da Flora. In an age of slick spaces and slicker food, Gaspar and partner Mary Beth Marks are nurturing a lost art: "Dining is a social event and a sensual ritual – it's supposed to be savored." Not that you'd want to rush through sweet potato gnocchi sparked with bacon and swathed in sherry cream, squid-ink risotto or pork chop served with wine-soaked figs. The meal's leisurely pace promotes lingering, from the hot, salt-crusted focaccia that starts things off to the blood-orange granita that marks its sweet close.

32 Baraka

Both the food and décor can be loosely defined as "Moorish Moderne." Small, lush and painted in saturated shades of blood-red, paprika and eggplant, Baraka is illuminated at lunch by sunlight slanting through the windows and at dinner by dozens of flickering candles – some set back into arched niches and dropped into a large, wrought-iron chandelier, others set directly on top of the copper-topped tables. From the same team responsible for nearby Chez Papa (page 41), which shares Ola Fendert as executive chef, Baraka takes the San Francisco fetish for small plates and turns its gaze towards North Africa (via Spain). Ushered in by a bowl of spiced cashews – and perhaps a glass of citrusy, white sangria – a meal might lead from a crunchy fava bean salad with sugar peas and asparagus spiked with mint to a friture of anchovies with fennel to a saffrony rabbit tagine studded with green olives and preserved lemon. Lunch brings sandwiches, such as cinnamon-scented merguez with harissa aioli. And sweet mint tea served in tiny Moroccan glasses with floating pine nuts makes a lovely coda.

60 **Slanted Door**

4 Ferry Building

When the Slanted Door first opened in a Mission district storefront, Charles Phan's fresh executions of Vietnamese food caught fire, and made reservations as rare as hen's teeth. Now his restaurant has moved to the Ferry Building and the original space is expanding into a kind of Vietnamese noodle house. In his expansive new digs on the water, Phan and his staff (which numbers thirteen family members) have the space to accommodate more diners and the fish tanks he's been longing for, which means even more of the seasonally inspired dishes with which Phan made his mark: fresh spring rolls filled with shrimp, pork, mint and peanut sauce, Meyer Ranch shaking beef with garlic, caramelized chicken clay pot, gulf prawns with baby bok choy. Even desserts get the Phan treatment – sweet black rice pudding with fresh papaya and coconut sauce and a mascarpone mousse with gingerbread cake and persimmons.

FRESH OFF THE BOAT

88 **Swan Oyster Depot**

6 1517 Polk Street

When craving a taste of the sea, San Franciscans do not go to Fisherman's Wharf. *Ever*. Since 1912, they've trekked to this fish-shop-cum-oyster-bar, joined the almost perennial line, perched atop one of 18 seats at the marble counter, ordered an icy beer or glass of wine, and waited expectantly. Sal Sancimino bought Swan in 1946, and his five sons now run the tiny storefront with a cheerful blend of humor and showmanship. True to its name, Swan serves oysters – from sweet and fruity Kumamotos to meaty Miyagis – as well as smoked salmon and whitefish (a breakfast favorite with crusty sourdough), Boston clam chowder, seafood cocktails and salads mounded with any combination of shrimp, prawns, Dungeness crab and lobster, and topped with a choice of dressings and condiments – from the house Louie to oil and vinegar, squeeze of lemon, hot sauce and horseradish. Although the shop closes at five thirty, everything is available to take away – many a casual picnic and swank dinner party has its origins chez Swan.

60 Jai Yun
36 923 Pacific Avenue

The décor approximates the "before" shot in a reality makeover show, but you're here for the artistry of chef–owner Ji Nei', an émigré from Nanjing, and his dégustation menu of small, delicately flavored, scantly-sauced dishes that emerge from the kitchen in endless progression like something out of a culinary *Sorcerer's Apprentice.* Wrote Olivia Wu in the *San Francisco Chronicle,* "Nei' is the find that every food lover hopes to stumble across once…his sense of culture and authenticity remains intact." Shopping in Chinatown daily, Nei' cures his own meats, pickles his vegetables and does most of the prep. After myriad cold appetizers – a kind of Chinese meze – the meal starts in earnest: drunken chicken simmered in wine, velvet abalone, tangerine beef fried with citrus peel and chilis, a whole fish scattered with shredded seaweed, skewered basil mushrooms, or a tureen of soup redolent of the sea. No wonder other chefs address him as "sifu," or master, and that the restaurant has the nickname "Chinese Laundry," an allusion to Thomas Keller's legendary (and impossible-to-get-into) prix-fixe restaurant in Yountville.

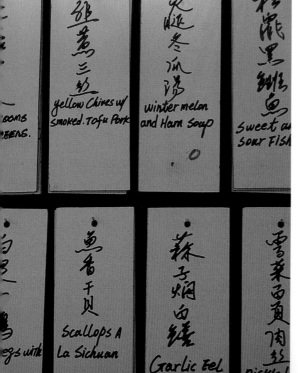

32 La Taqueria
24 2889 Mission Street

Everybody in San Francisco has an opinion about which taco joint reigns supreme. La Taqueria may not have the most ambitious menu, nor does it stay open the latest. The reason that local Latino families, club kids and everybody else has flocked here for almost thirty years is for the authentic food, which is always impeccably fresh, deeply flavorful and intensely satisfying. Waiting in line you can see the meat – *carne asada* (beef), *pollo* (shredded chicken simmered with chilis), *carnitas* (pork slowly cooked in its own fat), chorizo or tongue – being variously grilled, stewed, chopped and assembled to order into savory soft tacos or burritos (free of the rice filler prevalent at other places), and ponder whether to add pinto beans and whole chunks of avocado. Then escort your steaming plate, chips, salsa and icy beer or fruity agua fresca (cantaloupe, lime or strawberry) to one of the indoor picnic tables or out to the front patio to watch the street life unfold.

drink

Although it can feel as if mineral water is the libation of choice in this formerly hard-drinking town (especially at lunchtime), a perfectly stirred or shaken cocktail has never gone out of style. Some historic haunts, such as the Redwood Room and casbah-like Zam Zam, have been reanimated, while a new generation of modern lounges, such as 111 Minna and the beautifully appointed Rosewood, draw on the city's famously talented DJ pool to set the tone and provide the back beats. And any serious connoisseur of the liquid arts will hightail it to César, a tapas bar whose vast and varied listings include everything from eau to eaux-de-vie.

HOMAGE À PAGNOL

98 Café Fanny

1603 San Pablo Avenue

Named for Alice Waters' daughter Fanny (herself named for a character in Pagnol's famous Marseilles trilogy), this tiny café with a few outdoor tables has the air of a stand-up tabac in a small French village that's been suddenly dropped into the West Berkeley flatlands. Handmade tiles cover the floor, and the long zinc bar can accommodate about twenty people. The café au lait is served in bowls, the orange pressé is fresh, and it avoids feeling precious because everything is so good. In the morning there are perfect farm eggs, served with house preserves and levain toast from the legendary Acme bakery next door. Also made in-house is the now-famous Café Fanny Granola and buckwheat crepes that come sweet or savory – filled with fresh fruit or stuffed with ham and Gruyère. Lunch by way of Provence includes little Nice-style pizzas, a paté plate and an egg-salad sandwich topped with sundried tomatoes, anchovies and aioli, which are further enlivened by a glass of wine or the house kir. The Kermit Lynch Wine Merchant (page 165) flanks Fanny's other side, for a post-prandial peek at the Bandols.

CASTRO CROSSROADS

44 Café Flore

27 2298 Market Street

An institution sitting at a busy Castro district crossroads, Café Flore's wraparound, wind-protected patio provides maximum exposure as well as a vantage point for checking out the continuous procession of humanity. The ordering line, which snakes down a long Victorian-era counter, provides more opportunities for looking over the local talent. Open from early till late, the Flore is where you come to gossip over steamed eggs and espresso the morning after an endless night (perhaps with a ½-liter of the house mimosas – orange juice and sparkling wine), grab a salad and Hefeweizen, or nurse a Cinzano while cruising for a missed connection. The café recently changed hands, with no change in the ambience of this former gas station – it still has a corrugated metal roof, exposed structural bracing, and wisteria vines that sometimes triumph over traffic fumes.

Since this destination bakery (which migrated from rural Marin County to the Mission district) added a wine bar with more than a dozen interesting offerings available by the glass, people seem to dig in their heels for hours. Elizabeth Prueitt oversees the pastry side of things, while husband Chad Robertson bakes the wonderfully chewy and crusty country loaves featured in the namesake tartines. Breakfast is sweet or savory, with such confections as orange and cinnamon buns, buttermilk scones and a rich gougère of Gruyère and herbs. Hot pressed sandwiches include inspired combinations such as pecorino and almonds crushed with olive oil, lemon and sage. And dessert is an all-day affair, with a rotating roster of fresh fruit Bavarians and tarts filled with almond or rose geranium cream, Mexican wedding cookies, lemon and fresh bergamot bars, a caramel-kissed banana-cream pie and cakes festooned with fresh flowers.

32 **Farley's**

33 1315 18th Street

There's usually a claque of vintage motorcycles in various states of repair outside, with people lounging on the steps, at tables, on the sidewalk and inside this funky, spacious café carved out of a Victorian-era cottage. As the Potrero Hill neighborhood upscales all around, owner Roger Hilyard gamely resists the urge to tart things up. The espresso drinks are perfect (just don't utter the words "non-fat"), the tea is all loose-leaf, and there's rotating art on the walls and backgammon and Scrabble on the shelves (clearly, lingering is encouraged). You're even allowed to bring in food from the take-out place next door. But the coup-de-grâce at Farley's is the fully stocked magazine stand where you're left in peace to peruse everything from fashion and design porn to literary journals and obscure automotive rags. And nobody flinches when you drag them back to your table. Starbucks could learn a thing or two....

60 Caffe Trieste
31 601 Vallejo Street

When the Giotta family opened Caffe Trieste in 1956 in the heart of North Beach, the West Coast gained its first espresso coffeehouse. Situated on a strip of sidewalk off the Columbus Avenue hoopla, Trieste attracts locals, visitors and refugees from other 'hoods, some here for a quick cup, others entrenched long enough to produce entire screenplays as the aroma of the house-roasted coffee beans hangs in the air. Definitely, there's a difference between weekday regulars and the weekend crowd. Every Saturday at 2 pm the Giotta family jam gets underway (and drink prices temporarily rise), as Papa Gianni and wife Ida sing traditional Italian songs and opera, sister Sonia segues into country-and-western, and brother Fabio squeezes the accordion – a congenial familial free-for-all.

60 Imperial Tea Court
38 1411 Powell Street

The dark wooden interior with square tables, lanterns, hooks for birdcages and antique tea counter was appointed by visiting Chinese craftsmen who created an alternate universe where time slows down and even moves backwards. Roy Fong – tea master and Daoist Priest – and his wife, Grace, established the first traditional teahouse in America to revive a practice that dates to the Tang Dynasty. To order a cup of Monkey Picked Tekuanyin, Imperial Dragon Well or organic Darjeeling is to learn that each blend has its own brewing process. Tea is served in the *gaiwan*, or covered teacup style, in which a lid is used to strain leaves as one sips, with accompaniments such as ginger-roasted almonds and peanut cookies. All varieties are available to purchase, as are the "purple sand" teapots – some of Fong's own design – from the historic pottery workshops of Yixing. At their outpost at the Ferry Building, the tea presentations are joined by tea-steamed dim sum and other delicacies.

14 **Garden Court and Pied Piper Bar**

30 The Palace Hotel, 2 New Montgomery Street

The Palace opened in 1875 aiming to be the world's largest and most luxurious hotel; today its grand façade conceals two historic places to pause for refreshment. The stained-glass dome of the Garden Court crowns the hotel's former carriage entrance, now a plant-filled atrium (and official landmark) with leaded crystal chandeliers and marble columns where one can take breakfast, lunch and Saturday afternoon tea. More clubby is the Pied Piper Bar, named for the Maxfield Parrish mural painted in 1909 for

the hotel's post-earthquake reopening. (The temblor reportedly caused a fleeing, towel-clad Caruso to quip, "I will never set foot in San Francisco again.") Its mahogany bar and marble-topped tables are a match for the top-shelf Martinis, the regrettable addition of televisions being the only obvious nod to modernity.

88 **Tonga Room**

1 The Fairmont Hotel, 950 Mason Street

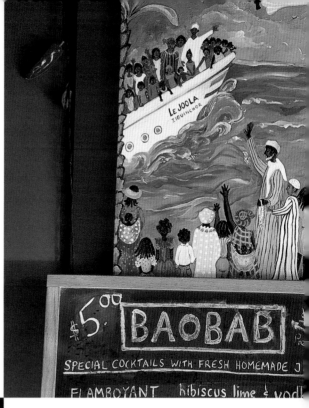

Easter Island meets Disneyland at the Tonga Room, a tiki lounge in the Fairmont Hotel that sits atop Nob Hill. This ersatz Polynesian pleasure dome evolved from an indoor swimming pool into a simulated tropical paradise after World War II, when soldiers returned bearing photos of the exotic South Pacific. Today it attracts a mélange of ironists, business types, seniors and connoisseurs of camp, with its thatched roofs, fertility totems, regular thunderstorms and brightly colored, umbrella-shaded cocktails of the rum-coconut-fruit-juice variety, such as the "Bora Bora Horror" and glowing "Blue Hawaii." Some libations come served in hollowed-out pineapples, others in faux-carved ceramic vessels, all topped with arrangements of fruit and flora worthy of Carmen Miranda. The house band plays from a boat that floats across the lagoon as the uninhibited take to the dance floor, part of a Spanish galleon run aground. Happy hour is the best time to sample a grog before departing for dryer climes.

SENEGALESE BEATS AND BREWS

32 **Bissap Baobab**

20 2323 Mission Street

Shaded by palm fronds, this Senegalese watering hole named for a majestic native tree and symbol of life is the place to play ex-pat in Africa. Perch at the bar and wash down a plate of fried plantains or pastelle (fish pastries) with cocktails with lovely names – L'hiver (lemon vodka, midori, ginger), Saff (gin, ginger, grapefruit), Fleur (tamarind, ginger, whisky) – while twitching to infectious West-African beats. Food is cheap and cheerful, with grilled and stewed meats and vegetables cooked in tangy sauces such as peanut-based mafe. Chef–owner–DJ Marco Olivier Senghor (cousin of the late Leopold Senghor, former president of Senegal and Nobel-nominated poet) arrived in the Mission district via France and is friends with a cadre of musicians, including Spearhead's Michael Franti, who records spoken word pieces here. Around the corner, Little Baobab (3388 19th Street) offers the same spicy island drinks with Creole fare and dancing (to DJ Marco, *bien sur*) on the weekends.

PAST PERFECT

14 **Redwood Room**

16 Clift, 495 Geary Street

When Schrager and Starck set about renovating and reimagining this 1933 Art Déco landmark as part of their mega-makeover of the Clift Hotel, preservationists (many of whom had not stepped foot in the place for eons) held a candlelight vigil. They needn't have worried. The genius of the place has been respected and the cobwebs swept away. The towering redwood-paneled walls, crafted from a single 2,000-year-old tree, were unmolested, and the bar (which was rotting) is surrounded in illuminated, hand-etched mirrored glass. Many of the furnishings and materials share the reddish-brown tones of the walls and bar, creating a calm, monochromatic setting that bridges the decades. Plasma screens display the old reproduction Klimts, which now morph into the works of digital artists, and a DJ has replaced the piano. It's a lovely (if pricey) place to lounge with a lavender or litchi Martini (especially weeknights, to avoid the savage hordes), while indulging in a little alcohol-fueled remembrance of things past.

DREAMING OF SAN SEBASTIAN

98 **César**

1515 Shattuck Ave

César's menu of libations runs to 25 pages, while its 20 Catalan tapas fit neatly on a page. The sophisticated, high-ceilinged room nestles next to Chez Panisse (it was founded by a few alums), and has a long tiled zinc bar from which to view the action. In the center is a communal pine table made from floorboards salvaged from a London warehouse, and on sultry nights, the windows open to extend the room onto the sidewalk. Among the wines, spirits, artisan ciders and beers and cocktails are tasting flights of everything from tequilas, single-malt scotches, grappas and eaux-de-vies to Polish vodkas and single-village mezcals. Executive chef Maggie Pond is a veteran of San Sebastian and Barcelona, and her tapas and bocadillos (most under $7) are savory companions for the liquid treats: tombo spiked with chunky romesco, a *cazuela* of salt cod and potato, homemade chorizo with chickpeas, crispy potatoes topped with herbs and sea salt and sweet, tiny cookies that cry out for a glass of dessert wine or port.

STYLISH CHILL SPACE

60 **Rosewood**

39 732 Broadway

There's no sign out front, so look for the anonymous steel door bookmarked by storefront bays along Broadway where North Beach and Chinatown kiss. Named for its walls of Bolivian rosewood, this intimate DJ lounge with white Formica bartop, salvaged Thonet barstools and low leather sofas is owned by Jon Gasparini and Greg Lindgren, the team who dreamed up 15 Romolo (a popular nearby speakeasy in the old Basque Hotel). Rosewood draws more of a chilled-out crowd, here to drink well-blended cocktails and converse as electronica and French hip-hop play through the orb-shaped Italian speakers that float from the ceiling like giant olives. Illuminated by George Nelson pendants, the back room is a venue for art exhibits, indie films and Hong Kong action flicks, and opens onto a garden patio that feels like an urban oasis. To get in the mood, one might sample one of the many rare Chinese elixirs stocked by the bar – but be forewarned, they're definitely an acquired taste.

32 · 22 **Laszlo**

2526 Mission Street

Sharing a name with bad-boy character in Godard's *Breathless* and walls (and a prodigious wine cellar) with the Foreign Cinema restaurant, Laszlo has cultivated its own devoted following of lounge-worshippers – some there for the expert mixologists, others for the ever-rotating array of beats. The multilevel industrial décor (glass, steel, concrete) is softened by candles, house concoctions such as the Ruby and Sapphire (Bombay Sapphire gin, muddled lime and pomegranate syrup imported from Iran), and an admirable champagne selection. Before nine o'clock, the bartender spins everything from The Hives to P. J. Harvey and The Coral, at a volume that encourages conversation; later, a DJ rolls in and unleashes the flavor of the night – from downtempo to hip-hop, breaks, Euro-techno, or spoken word. An added bonus: bar food comes from the Foreign Cinema kitchen, so you can graze on salt cod, foie gras, or a platter of fruits de mer (oysters, clams, prawns, crab) while musing over why they don't make films the way they used to and what happened to Godard after *Weekend*.

14 · 31 **111 Minna Gallery**

111 Minna Street

In a cavernous space contained behind giant stable doors, 111 Minna's founders created an urban hybrid. The art gallery opens at noon, with op-art installations that embrace all media, including surfboards. Happy hour kicks in at five o'clock (overseen by a monolithic metal dragonfly hanging over the bar), and from then the space might morph into a screening room for new animation or a dance club where DJs spin into the night. Music runs the post-rave gamut – you might hear garage, dub, South African beats and retro house all in looping succession. Deservedly legendary are Wednesday's long-running Qoöl parties, where Looq label DJs such as Spesh and Jondi ramp up the progressive house at six and wind down at nine, in time to totter off to dinner. Financial planners, professional hipsters, well-coiffed Marina types and pierced and jaded Mission kids find common ground in the music and peak together during a happy hour turned ecstasy hour – even without the mood-enhancing drugs.

ART DÉCO DANCE CLUB

60 Bimbo's 365 Club
29 1025 Columbus Avenue

With one of the best sound systems in the city and a storied past, Bimbo's is a magical place to hear live music over civilized cocktails at a cloth-draped table. Michael Cerchiai runs the club founded by his grandfather on Market Street in 1931 (it later moved to its current location at the foot of Russian Hill in North Beach), and the stage where Rita Cansino hoofed (before she became Rita Hayworth) and Duke Ellington conducted now hosts folks like the White Stripes, Coldplay, Cake, Talvin Singh, Zero 7, Aimee Mann, the Tiger Lilies, St Germain and the incomparable David Johansen and the Harry Smiths. During high-octane shows, tables are cleared to make room for dancing, while acoustic performances retain the intimacy of a 1940s night club. The original Art Déco detailing and fixtures remain, as do restroom attendants, who offer everything from towels to shave tonics. Even Dolfina, the famous "Girl in the Fishbowl," still makes occasional appearances in the club's Continental Lounge. (Check local listings or their website for shows.)

HISTORIC HAUNT

60 Tosca Café
18 242 Columbus Avenue

Not a lot has changed inside Tosca since 1911, from the huge rococo La Pavoni espresso makers hissing on top of the bar to the antique cash register, faded mural of Venice, and picture gallery of opera stars, who also appear on the jukebox (three songs for a quarter). As proprietor Jeannette Etheridge numbers legions of artists among her friends, one might bump into Sam Shepard, Tom Waits, Sean Penn, Francis Coppola or Mikhail Baryshnikov on any given night (such luminaries have access to the hallowed private room with pool table). But others are allowed to imbibe their Martinis and grappas here as well, either at the blood-red booths and tables in the back or at the long mahogany bar, where glasses are lined up for the house "cappuccino" – a chocolate- and brandy-infused beverage that slips down a tad too easily.

32 Lone Palm
 14 3394 22nd Street

A single palm tree and neon sign mark the entrance to this bar, which happens to be a fine place for an assignation. Sitting on a residential street in relative anonymity, the bar's lighting is low, the candlelight flattering, and the retro-noirish ambience softer than one finds at most of the edgier Mission district dives (where tongue studs must practically be shown at the door to gain entry). Huddling at the cloth-draped tables over a couple of icy perfect Manhattans or Martinis deep enough to dive into, you can actually hear your companion over the cocktail music or live piano. A flickering television shows classic films (from *Planet of the Apes* to *Casablanca*) with the sound turned off, and the Egyptian bas-reliefs appear to have been borrowed from a 1940s film set.

OPIUM DEN AMBIENCE
60 Li Po
40 916 Grant Avenue

Named for one of the great poets of the Tang Dynasty (who celebrated love and nature as well as drink), this dark, cavernous bar with the huge, tattered lantern and golden Buddha feels more like an opium den (which it was reputed to be) than the scene of a poetry slam. In fact, the only slamming you'll hear, day and night, is that of the dice cups onto the bar, wielded by the old Chinese men from the neighborhood who seem oblivious to the comings and goings of upstart imbibers and migrating hipsters. Once a hangout for seamen on leave in the old Barbary Coast days (when it was not uncommon for an inebriated sailor to be "shanghaied" and wake up in servitude on a foreign ship), it has large red-backed booths shrouded in a darkness that encourages illicit activity, and its cocktails are honest, decent and strong.

44 **Persian Aub Zam Zam**

36 1633 Haight Street

The mythology surrounding Bruno Mooshei, the Zam Zam's erstwhile curmudgeonly owner, can overshadow this gemlike bar, built by his father in 1941 with Moorish minarets and Gothic windows that cast colored lights into the interior. (Known locally as the "Martini nazi," Bruno was famous for tossing people out if they dared to order a vodka Martini.) Sitting smack in the heart of the Haight Ashbury a few blocks from Golden Gate Park, the lounge became surrounded by head shops as the Summer of Love approached ("hippies" also ranked high on Bruno's list of annoyances), but never lost its allure even as he became increasingly bitter with each passing decade. Happily, new owner Bob Clarke hasn't touched the ersatz Arabian Nights décor, nor the jukebox (last changed in 1955) filled with the likes of Ella, Frank and Louis, and he graciously shakes icy Martinis and cosmos for all polite comers, whether they're sitting at the semicircular bar or at one of the tables tucked into a corner. In true Bruno tradition, however, only the ladies get the groovy cocktail napkins.

shop

Labels and logos loudly flaunted do not have much currency in San Francisco, which has generally been more interested in starting new movements than slavishly following established trends. Instead, the Bay Area is more of a hunting ground for the well crafted and the wonderfully quirky — be it a rare stone pillow from Koichi Hara's Japonesque Gallery, one of Smith Williams's embroidered men's shirts or a limited-edition sneaker from Huf. While a few shops (such as Metier) are must-detours within the big-name maze of Union Square, many more are nestled into neighborhoods, where lower rents allow for creative endeavors outside the corporate boxes.

SARTORIAL MIX MASTER

14

Metier

 355 Sutter Street

Sheri Evans's sun-washed shop has been swimming against the downtown tide of cookie-cutter chains for 15 years. Women come for Anna Molinari's dolce vita dresses and Mayle and James Coviello's vintage detailing, and the cream of the home-grown crop. Metier was one of the first to stock Suzi Johnson's Souchi line of soft wool sweaters woven in shades like wisteria, sage and safety orange, and her knitted bikinis with boy-shorts bottoms, and is still the only place to find local legend Wynn Smith's idiosyncratic collection "Wink" (Morticia Adams-meets-Mrs Moneypenny). Evans also nurtures Bay Area jewelers who end up going big time: Becky Kelso's Eastern-exotic chandelier earrings sparkle beside Janine Payer's silver pieces engraved with tiny quotations from Zola to Chekhov. And there is nowhere else in the city to try on (designer to the stars) Cathy Waterman's garden-inspired platinum-and-diamond rings, earrings, bracelets and chokers, famously patterned with flowers and trailing vines punctuated with the occasional colored stone, as lyrical and delicate as calligraphy from a medieval text.

Siblings Chris and Ben Ospital opened MAC more than twenty years ago, in a tiny space that attracted a disproportionate amount of attention for its inspired, sometimes irreverent mix of left-coast and international talent. Newly relocated in the Hayes Valley, MAC remains a kind of social hub and information portal to what's happening around town and beyond. It's well stocked for, say, attorneys who ride Vincents – with Armand Basi's sharp suits with bespoke details and a fantasia of ties from Romeo Gigli. Freelance types pore over luxe-proletariat workshirts and cashmere from hrm and San Franciscan Sergio Davila's mohair knits, woven in his native Peru – which complement original Antwerp Six member Walter van Beirendonck's twisted folkloric prints. For women, locals Lemon Twist pay homage to Courrèges in fog-weight wool skirts and jackets (some available in infant sizes), and Mission-gal Dema Grim's Mod Squad profiles are run up in MAC-exclusive liberty prints. Miller et Bertaux's sweeping wool coats and Dirk van Saene and A.F. Vandervorst's Bloomsbury-on-acid separates are ideally suited to the city's seasonless climate and iconoclastic bent.

14 1 Gimme Shoes

50 Grant Avenue • 2358 Fillmore Street •
416 Hayes Street

In a city not awash with brilliant footwear (some blame the
hills, others the weather), the Gimme Shoes shops owned
by Jerry Warwick and Leigh Stackpole shine like beacons.
Broody Belgians Dries Van Noten and Véronique
Branquinho perch cheek-by-jowl next to Miu Miu, Helmut
Lang and Costume National, with space devoted to well-
priced lines such as Moma, who makes a hit boot every
season, and all-American Fryes. All heel heights are
represented, from stilettos to Paul Smith's quirky court
shoes and foot-molding leather sandals by former San
Franciscan Jutta Newman, whose leather totes in saturated
shades of acid green, turquoise and brick hang on the
wall. Also embracing the comfort principle is the new
wave of athletics shoes – Yohji's Y3 trainers for Adidas
rendered in cool treated leathers and Neil Barrett's street
shoe hybrids for Puma. And among the eye candy at the
counter are Sigerson Morrison's purses in soda-pop colors.

CLEAN CUTS
14 12 Diana Slavin

3 Claude Lane

Diana Slavin began selling her cleancut designs to local
boutiques soon after moving from New York years ago, but
she really sewed up her reputation as a haberdasher at her
atelier on tiny Claude Lane, a moody, mewslike alley in
the heart of downtown that's home to a café and a couple
boutiques. There is nothing mannish about Slavin's coats,
jackets, skirts and trademark trousers, rather she has a
master tailor's devotion to fabrics and drape and design
details that arise organically – a twist here, a tuck there –
rather than being added as embellishment. Slavin works
directly with mills in Italy and Japan to select the wools,
cottons and linens for her collections, which range from
neutrals such as black, tobacco and stone to lovely muddy
blues. Neisha Crosland and Jane Wheeler's scarves and
shoes by Robert Clergerie share Slavin's bias towards
innate artistry over obvious glam.

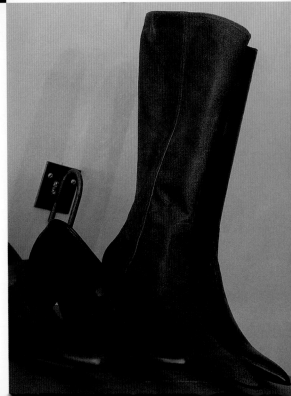

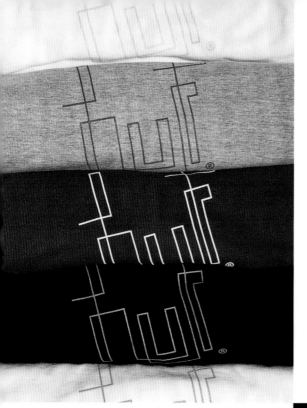

MENSWEAR LUMINARY
88 Smith Williams

14 1827 Union Street

Spending seven years as an investment banker in New York did not quash either Smith Williams's soft, North Carolina accent or his huge design talent. This Savile-row-meets-Milan haberdashery for men is filled with his Italian-tailored creations that have a European fit and metrosexual appeal. Button-down shirts have op-art prints, exaggerated cuffs or three tiny, colored buttons in place of one. And Williams overlays embroidery to visual and textural effect – a military-style shirt might be embellished with a single flower or dragons running down the sleeves, or be covered in what appear to be paramecium. Suits are made from touch-friendly fabrics like wool and cashmere, white moleskin, orange velvet and raw silk, many with a choice of tapered or low-rise, fuller-bottomed pants (a nice match for his distressed ponyskin belts).

SKATER CULTURE
14 Huf

20 808 Sutter Street

Professional skateboarder Keith Hufnagel has long been obsessed with rare sneakers. Now he doesn't have to look very far, because he and his wife, Anne, sell them. Hufnagel collaborated on a Nike style of which only 808 pairs exist – a play on Huf's address – and he stocks hand-embellished Jeremy Scott Adidas along with stores such as Colette. Vault by Vans are old school high-tops re-imagined by designers such as Louella and Rebecca Taylor in hot pink checks and fresh florals. Much of the streetwear – Alife, Supreme, Annex – at the new Huf clothing boutique next door is designed by skater pals, as are the clay sculptures by local legend Mark Gonzalez. "We were worried before the store opened," says Anne. "Then, on the first day, a line of Japanese kids greeted us at the door: 'We're ready for shopping now!'"

FOOD MECCA
| 60 | **Ferry Building Marketplace**
| 2 | Market Street at Embarcadero

If San Francisco's religion is food, then the Ferry Building can only be Mecca. Built in 1898 with full Victorian pomp, it was a beacon for ships and a hub for commuters before the bridges siphoned off travelers and an unsightly freeway cut off the waterfront (the '89 earthquake took care of the freeway). The lighted clocktower was modeled on the belltower of Seville's cathedral and the building's scale was almost as grand – with a nave running beneath a 660-foot-long, 45-foot wide (201 x 13.8-meter), steel-trussed skylight and a marble mosaic floor. Following an extensive restoration, the building is now a homage to artisanal edibles. A stroll along the nave turns up tasty bivalves (Hog Island Oyster Company), world-class cheeses (Cowgirl Creamery), pain levain (Acme Bread Company), handmade gelato (Ciao Bella), a seafood counter and much more, as well as restaurants such as nouvelle Vietnamese Slanted Door (page 142). With water transit on the rise, commuters can again walk through to catch their ferries, this time picking up dinner along the way.

ORGANICALLY GROWN
| 60 | **Farmers' Market**
| 3 | Behind the Ferry Building

The Center for Urban Education about Sustainable Architecture (CUESA) runs the Farmers' Market behind the Ferry Building on an outdoor plaza overlooking the bay. On Saturdays, well over a hundred farmers and food producers offer everything from fava beans, heirloom tomatoes and morels to free-range chicken, wild smoked salmon, lemon marmalade and doughnut muffins (from the nirvana-inducing Downtown Bakery in Healdsburg). It's as much a social gathering as a culinary event, with chef-spotting a spectator sport – from Jamie Oliver, in town for a book tour, to Zuni Café's Judy Rodgers. Some come not to shop but to tuck into a meal from one of the half-dozen food stands, such as Primavera, whose authentic Mexican cuisine includes such delicacies as shrimp and snapper tostadas de ceviche, and Hayes Street Bar and Grill's succulent fried oyster po' boy sandwiches. All of this abundance, strangely enough, is overseen by a central statue of Mahatma Gandhi, surveying the scene impassively, staff in hand.

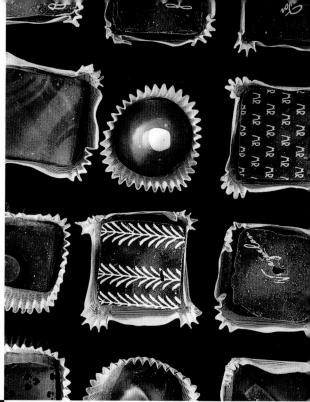

98 Kermit Lynch Wine Merchant
1605 San Pablo Avenue

When Kermit Lynch opened his shop three decades ago (one of his earliest customers was Chez Panisse), he couldn't know he would one day be decorated by the French government (*Chevalier de l'Ordre de Mérite Agricole*) or deemed among "the most influential wine personalities of the last 20 years" (Robert Parker). Importer, merchant, author (*Adventures on the Wine Route: A Wine Buyer's Tour of France*, considered among the best books on wine written in English), and producer (Les Palières, in Gigondas), Lynch found his niche exploring little-trod French wine routes and crusading for the old artisanal methods. He abhors filtering and the big, bombastic brews that often result, and is equally leery of numerical rating systems that favor fat, jammy wines over vintages of individuality, character and finesse. What you'll find in his shop are selections that celebrate the concept of *terroir*; what you won't find is anything from California. The staff are equally evangelical, whether recommending a very affordable Corsican white or something much more rarefied.

CANDY COUTURIER
60 Recchiuti Confections
5 Ferry Building, no. 30

He's been compared to Picasso (*Gourmet*) and a "detail-obsessed Mies van der Rohe in Candy Land" (*Real Simple*), but avant-garde chocolatier Michael Recchiuti is an original. A pastry chef by métier, he melds classic French and Belgian techniques with the San Franciscan love of experimentation. Herbs, spices, tea and fruit are fodder for his confections, which are sparked by everything from rose-geranium oil to Earl Grey, star anise and pink peppercorns. Combinations that might sound odd – bitter chocolate ganache infused with fresh tarragon leaves and candied grapefruit peel – taste fresh and inspired once they hit the tongue. Recchiuti even tweaks S'Mores, that classic American camping treat – although his handmade marshmallows, graham crackers and 85% bittersweet bar evoke Proustian memories of some idealized trip from our dreams.

44 Dark Garden

6 321 Linden Street

"Our clients range from blushing bride to brazen dominatrix," says Autumn Carey-Adamme, who fashions exactingly fitted and meticulously crafted corsets for formal and fetish wear and everything in between. "Oh, and Marilyn Manson!" she adds. Well, who couldn't use a little extra structure and support in his or her life? "Creatrix" Carey-Adamme and her crew offer three levels of the steel-boned beauties: ready-to-wear, custom and couture – the latter involving a minimum of 12 individual measurements and requiring a three-month lead time. And choices abound. Laces or hooks? Satin, brocade or shiny, shiny leather? Sweetheart Victorian or under-the-bust Edwardian? Amazon, Arch-rival or Empress? While you browse at the funky Hayes Valley atelier, aural stimulation is provided by the hum of sewing machines and the *thumpa thumpa* of grommets being set into fabric.

98

MILLINERY ARTS
Zazu & Violet's Hats

11 1790 Shattuck Avenue

While Sydney Turkshek's hats are not worn by the Queen at Royal Ascot, they do top luminaries stateside, including actress Nicole Kidman and Chez Panisse chef Alice Waters, whose cloche collection is prodigious (and whose restaurant is just down the road). Named for Turkshek's two daughters, Zazu & Violet's hats are sold at boutiques and Barneys, New York, but there is something about sitting in her cozy millinery shop and trying on the hand-sewn, -blocked and -embellished boaters, berets and wide-brimmed hats that feels straight out of Colette. Some are wrought from vintage (but virgin) straw that has a warm, natural patina impossible to duplicate with new material. Others are made of corded rayon braid in muted tones of wine, celery, lapis, tobacco and ink and ornamented with French ribbons and antique decorations from Eastern Europe, at once vaguely vintage and terribly *au courant*.

BEAT BOOKS

60 City Lights Bookseller & Publisher

21 261 Columbus Avenue

Although the Bohemian North Beach of 1953 that spawned City Lights may be a world away from today's high-rent 'hood, the nation's first all-paperback bookstore remains a place where literature and politics make fine bedfellows (as a sign explains, "Printer's ink is the greatest explosive"). And it's a combination lightning rod and conscience for the country: "In a time when the dominant TV-driven consumer culture would seem to result in the 'dumbing down' of America, City Lights is a finger in the dike holding back the flood of unknowing," explains poet, painter and founder Lawrence Ferlinghetti. Some of the early denizens – Jack Kerouac, William Burroughs, Lenny Bruce – are departed. But Allen Ginsberg's "Howl" remains the publishing arm's bestseller, half a century after Ferlinghetti defended it against obscenity charges. A new mural outside the store reproduces one painted by the Mayan community in Chiapas that was destroyed by the Mexican army. Inside is a rich repository of poetry, fiction, criticism, philosophy, 'zines and copious works in translation – as Vaclav Havel exclaimed upon visiting the store, "They have my book!"

SCENT SENSUALIST

14 Henri Baumann Les Parfums

7 210 Post Street, Suite 511

This room with pistachio green-walls and 18th-century chairs is the sole American outpost of Parfum Henry Jacques, the last house to formulate its 2,000 perfumes (100 rose varieties alone) without alcohol, animal oils or chemicals. Sébastien Baumann, proprietor and master "nose," is a matchmaker whose métier is scent rather than love, although the one may lead to the other. Baumann paired Madonna with Salalah Night (myrrh, Indian jasmine, Oman roses) and made a lilac-redolent blend for Lourdes. During a consultation he offers whiffs of precious essences such as O'od, derived from the agar tree. How did this Alsace native end up in San Francisco? "I've always loved the West – it's where I feel happy." Indeed, his citrusy "California" is a fittingly fresh and optimistic homage.

EXQUISITE EPHEMERA

98 Addison Endpapers

6397 Telegraph Avenue

"We make everything," explains Geneva Addison, who runs Addison Endpapers with her mother, Julie, and sister, Marina. They take original and found images – such as old bird and floral woodblock prints – punctuate them with stripes, dots and harlequin diamonds, then render the silk-screened papers into functional treasures: glass-topped boxes shaped like corsets, squares and bow-ties (the original antique once housed epaulets), stationery, and Pierrot-decorated containers made to store shimmery German mirror flake. Illustrated broadsides – such as one of a Jacques Prévert poem – are letter-pressed on the 115-year-old, human-powered press. Next door, Addison Antiques is a repository for "objects too numerous to mention, too strange to describe," from Chinese boxes to Victorian candymaking machines.

32 **Paxton Gate**

8 | 824 Valencia Street

"Everywhere you look should be a still life," says Paxton Gate proprietor and landscape designer Sean Quigley, who fills his surreal shop with startling and wonderful vignettes – like that huge, bird-eating tarantula mounted behind glass and the rare Buddha's Hand Citrus, whose fragrant fruit is shaped like a hand. Quigley describes his shop, named for naturalist Sir Joseph Paxton, who cultivated the giant Amazon water lily from seedlings and created London's Crystal Palace, as a repository for "rare and unusual oddities inspired by the garden and natural sciences." To us it looks like Martha Stewart as filmed by David Lynch. There are Japanese garden tools, vintage watering cans and preserved scarabs fighting over a ball of dung, painted glass taxidermy eyes and silver jewelry cast from the tiny bones of rats. An antiquarian apothecary kit offers up mercury and ergot (although the opium drawer is sadly empty). Not to worry, a freshly brewed cuppa is always on hand to take the edge off while perusing the art shows or hanging out in the garden with the carnivorous plants.

JEWEL BOX
44 **Alabaster**
12 597 Hayes Street

Now that Alabaster has expanded, Nelson Bloncourt finally has his Fortuny dream room filled with lanterns and fabrics and an al fresco home for his garden furniture, right in funky Hayes Valley. The new and vintage cream and tortoiseshell alabaster vessels and lamps for which the store was named fill a table, and a wall is stacked with luscious antique American creamware. Bloncourt often travels to Italy, and there are Fornasetti umbrellas, glass sea creatures by Venetian Bruno Amadi and 24-karat gold hand-hammered wedding bands from the Menichini Gioiellieri in Rome. Upholstered pieces by local designer Robert Trickey sit beside mid-century Lucite tables illuminated by Murano chandeliers custom-made for the shop – where, as Bloncourt admits, "necessities are few but wants are endless."

PRECIOUS GEMS
14 **De Vera**
4 29 Maiden Lane

At Federico De Vera's jewelbox of a jewelry shop, necklaces recline on vintage books, rings surround a 1910 glass vase by Fratelli Tosso and earrings rest atop Wiener-Werkstätte boxes. Indeed, most of the jewelry carries rumors of the old world. Third-century Greek and Roman intaglios, old Indian enamelwork and antique Persian filigree are among the raw materials. An etched woman's image from a Bakelite box is framed in gold and hung from antique threads; a crystal Victorian locket is embedded with rose-cut brown diamonds and paired with a strand of seed pearls and Venetian beads. "These are not reproductions," emphasizes David Morsa, who assists clients around the world. "Federico's art is in retaining the integrity of the piece while creating something utterly original."

EXOTIC BAZAAR

74 **Nest**

 2300 Fillmore Street
2340 Polk Street

The painted sign of the nest marks the shop; inside, sculpted wire chandeliers cradling glowing "eggs" hang from the high ceilings. Artists Judy Gilman and her daughter, Marcella Madsen (who painted the sign and interior details), transformed this former Victorian-era pharmacy into a cross-cultural bazaar that they think of as "very Bon Marché!" (The annex on Polk Street in Russian Hill is more devoted to larger-scale furnishings.) The

riotous mingling of East and West includes antique birdcages, Chinese lanterns, wine glasses made on 1920s molds, a Dutch ceramic tree-stump table, jewel-toned highball glasses, brightly striped teapots, Moroccan linens in dusty Maghreb hues, vintage saris, a shell-encrusted Victorian mirror, teas fragrant with fruit and Napoleon's preferred *savon*.

Everything in Koichi Hara's two-story gallery has a story to tell – from the bamboo letter opener to the 12th-century burned *Kannon* figure, from the rare *kogo* incense box to California sculptor Alma Allen's carvings out of wood, stone and bone – and is given the space to tell it. Hara, who has lived in Tokyo, Paris and Singapore, is a furniture designer and highly respected curator (he has sold works to the Asian Art Museum) as well as a master of *ma*, the breathing space that surrounds everything. His approach to the art of display and the way in which he treats each object with reverence and respect, have also been widely imitated. You can feel the Zen concept of *Wabi-Sabi* resonate within Hara's sanctuary, where there's a constant dialogue between ancient and modern, sometimes even within the same work – Hiromichi Iwashita's haunting wooden panels with undulating chisel marks, the abstract calligraphy of Yuichi Inoue, Hara's own hanging vase, which replaces bamboo with black steel pipe, and the basalt works of his friend, master carver Masatosi Izumi, who collaborated for 20 years with Isamu Noguchi.

Celebrates
Permanent Collection
New Asian Art Museum

74 **George**

8 2411 California Street
1844 Fourth Street, Berkeley

Fifteen years ago, a fox-terrier pup named George incited
his guardians to create the hip-looking pet products they
couldn't find elsewhere. Thus was born George, the store,
along with a burgeoning wholesale business that outfits
pets as far away as Japan. Designed with the warmth and
charm of an old-time general store, George is filled with
essentials like groovy striped turtleneck sweaters and
caps for dogs (with matching scarves for bipeds), quilted
rain slickers, tartan and studded collars, toys covered in
reissued Eames fabrics, vintage-type ticking beds, organic
catnip "cat trip" pillows, pet charms, old-fashioned enamel
bowls and baked-from-scratch treats, along with owner
Bobby Wise's enviable collection of canine and feline
paint-by-numbers. (Oh, and everything has been tested on
humans for animal consumption.)

"Colette meets Moss" offers Mark Lenox, defining Friend by referencing iconic stores in Paris and New York. "Too often there's a 'velvet rope' around great design. I wanted to create a hub where people could find out about design and San Francisco – in a warm, inviting environment." Friend's own designer is the charismatic Yves Béhar (featured in the Whitney Design Triennial), whose products for MINI_motion (driving watch, Samsonite messenger bag, Puma shoes) are here, along with home-oriented pieces such as his silver Lush Lily Tray. A stage of reclaimed wood curves up to form the back walls and concrete support columns are clad in acrylic, which bears a quote from third-century biographer Diongenes Laërtius: "All things are in common among friends." On the back wall, artists such as local photographer Todd Hito have a space to show two-dimensional work. Goods are a balance of local folk like Béhar, Offi and Publique Living and international – Canada's ZweiMineral, Splat from England, Johe Porzellan from Germany and Marc Newson.

Although Verdigris is in The Cannery at the foot of Leavenworth – and thus hovers precariously close to Fisherman's Wharf – it's a magnet for serious pottery collectors. Three owners make their studios here and show the work of more than forty artists in the adjacent gallery. Christa Assad, who studied with master potter Walter Ostrom as a Fulbright scholar in Canada after trekking round Europe and Asia, has earned a passel of awards for her wheelthrown vessels with strong, disciplined shapes (pitchers, cups, a sculptural teapot inspired by a 19th-century iron) and an ethos that's traceable to William Morris. Assad directs the rigor of her original field, aerospace engineering, to updating such traditional and purposeful forms as Japanese tea bowls and minimalist vases. Rae Dunn's clean, slab-and-coil-built pieces are often embossed with a single engaging word or design. And Mary Mar Keenan embellishes her more fantastical works with frankly decorative elements.

retreat

It's hard to imagine another urban center sitting in such easy proximity to so much natural beauty, whether one heads north to the wine regions of Napa or Sonoma or hugs the coast heading south. An hour and a half from the city center are rolling dunes and crashing waves, naturally heated mineral pools, rows of vineyards and acres of forests and meadows. While traffic to some of these retreats increases on summer weekends, they are surprisingly accessible most of the time, offering myriad possibilities for solitary wanderings and an opportunity to sample some of the region's bounty — from wild mushrooms to handcrafted cheeses — right at the source.

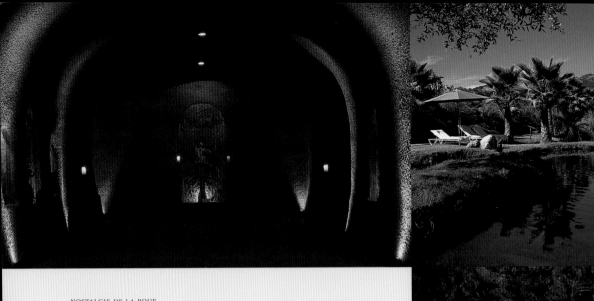

Calistoga: Taking the Waters

- Indian Springs
- Clos Pegase

The Wappo Indians were the first to discover the healing properties of the hot mineral springs and geysers bubbling up in the historic spa town of Calistoga, one and a half hours north of the Golden Gate Bridge. When the Merchant family refurbished every detail of the 140-year-old resort now known as Indian Springs (founded by California's first Gold Rush millionaire), they renamed it to honor the Napa Valley's original inhabitants. The 16-acre (6.5-hectare) grounds supply the magnesium- and calcium-rich volcanic ash used for the famous mud baths, and four geysers provide the steaming mineral water that fills the Olympic-sized pool. Eighteen charming, 1940s-style bungalows form a horseshoe around the property, with front porches, whitewashed plank floors, kitchens, down comforters and fluffy robes to wear to the pool and full-service spa. Out on the grass, Adirondack chairs, barbecues and hammocks are scattered among palm and olive trees.

Once you've relaxed, it's time for a drink. Dotting the Silverado Trail and Dunaweal Lane five minutes away are wineries such as Dutch Henry, Cuvaison, Sterling and Clos Pegase, whose pomo edifice was designed by Michael Graves as a "temple to wine and art" for proprietors Jan and Mitsuko Shrem. Their collection of 20th-century sculpture and painting is on display (the winery's label features Odilon Redon's *Winged Pegasus*), along with wine-related antiquities spanning 4,000 years. As devoted to his "inner Bacchus" as he is to the visual arts, Jan Shrem's self-described mission is "to achieve balance, harmony and symmetry in the classical Greek sense, avoiding the baroque concepts of high oak, high alcohol and high extract." It's a not unpleasant task to taste for yourself whether his mission has been accomplished.

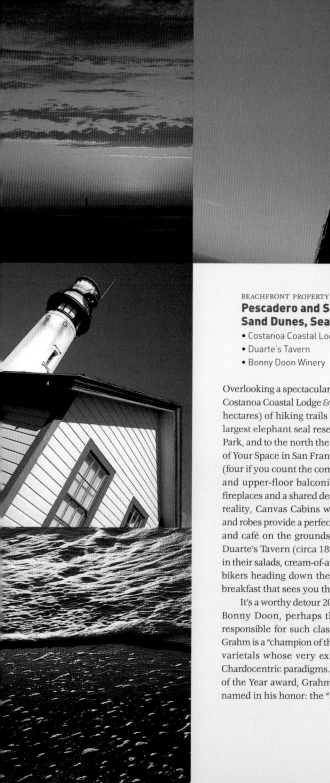

BEACHFRONT PROPERTY

Pescadero and Santa Cruz:
Sand Dunes, Sea Lions and Syrah

- Costanoa Coastal Lodge & Camp
- Duarte's Tavern
- Bonny Doon Winery

Overlooking a spectacular stretch of dunes and beaches an hour south of the city, Costanoa Coastal Lodge & Camp places four state parks and 30,000 acres (12,140 hectares) of hiking trails at your feet. To the south is Año Nuevo, the nation's largest elephant seal reserve, to the east stand the redwoods of Big Basin State Park, and to the north the Pigeon Point lighthouse. Designed by Jonathan Staub of Your Space in San Francisco, Costanoa offers three levels of accommodation (four if you count the comfy camping-site): rooms in the Lodge have fireplaces and upper-floor balconies with sweeping views; Douglas Fir Cabins offer fireplaces and a shared deck; and for those who prefer the idea of camping to the reality, Canvas Cabins with beds, heated mattress pads, down covers, lights and robes provide a perfect balance of nature and nurture. There's a general store and café on the grounds and in the nearby agricultural town of Pescadero, Duarte's Tavern (circa 1894) cooks local seafood and uses just-picked produce in their salads, cream-of-artichoke soup and fruit pies. A roadside legend among bikers heading down the coast, Duarte's serves the kind of big ol' American breakfast that sees you through an intensive day of hiking.

It's a worthy detour 20 miles (32 km) south and a few miles inland to bucolic Bonny Doon, perhaps the most eccentric winery in the hemisphere and responsible for such classic vintages as Le Cigare Volant. Proprietor Randall Grahm is a "champion of the strange and the heterodox, of the ugly duckling grape varietals whose very existence is threatened by the dominant Cabo- and Chardocentric paradigms." A winner of *Bon Appetit*'s Wine & Spirits Professional of the Year award, Grahm is perhaps the only winemaker to have an asteroid named in his honor: the "Rhoneranger."

Healdsburg: Heart of the Vine Country

- Hotel Healdsburg & Dry Creek Kitchen
- Jimtown Store

Sitting on a historic, Spanish-style plaza in Sonoma County, 67 miles (107 km) north of the city, Hotel Healdsburg is urbane, minimal and quietly luxe – yet feels like an organic part of this 140-year-old square. The three-story, 55-room hotel is broken up by allées and garden rooms below and connected with steel-and-glass bridges overhead. Instead of the usual tea-cozy-and-chintz country vernacular there are scattered Tibetan rugs, black teak furniture and a 60-foot (18-meter) pool surrounded by lavender, fig and olive trees. Inside the guestrooms are soaking tubs, private balconies and Frette linens. At Charlie Palmer's Dry Creek Kitchen, most of the raw ingredients come from local farms and purveyors and the wine list is similarly regional: all 500-plus offerings are from Sonoma County. Healdsburg sits happily at the confluence of three great appellations.

Heading towards one of those appellations, the Alexander Valley, leads to Jimtown, a general store built in 1893 and resurrected almost a century later by Carrie Brown and her late husband, John Werner (a partner in the New York specialty food store, The Silver Palate). Congenial and welcoming, it's filled with old-fashioned toys and candy, local products, groovy Americana and the best deli in the region – with fried Petaluma duck burgers, grilled dates with manchego and bacon and buttermilk pie to enjoy on the vine-covered patio or take away for a picnic with a bottle of the house wine.

Inverness: Storybook Hunting Lodge and Room to Roam

- Manka's Inverness Lodge
- Point Reyes National Seashore
- Hog Island Oysters

This wondrous old Arts and Crafts hunting lodge was built in 1917 in the hills of Inverness, a misty coastal Marin County village named by a nostalgic Scotsman. Within the main compound are eight comfortably rustic rooms, and three more down the road – including an 1850s cabin at the water's edge and a dramatic 1911 boathouse. The road sign for Manka's reads, "Honest Beds, Phenomenal Food," a sentiment echoed by more objective sources (the *Los Angeles Times* called it "By far one of the best restaurants in Northern California"). Almost everything that goes into the six-course menu has been grown, raised or caught within 15 minutes of the Lodge – from wild game to wild mushrooms and huckleberries.

As notable as Manka's is the land that surrounds it. The Point Reyes National Seashore is a wildly beautiful landmass replete with hundreds of miles of walking, biking and riding trails, and an opportunity to spot shorebirds, mountain lion and elk along the beaches, rolling meadows, redwood groves and hills.

A drive around Tomales Bay brings you to the tiny historic hamlet of Marshall and the Hog Island Oyster Company – suppliers to restaurants across the country. This working farm provides shucking knives, waterfront picnic tables and BBQs for a small fee, to enjoy oysters plucked fresh from their nearby beds.

contact

À Côté [131]
5478 College Avenue
Oakland, CA 94618
T   510 655 6469
F   510 655 6716
W www.citron-acote.com

**Absinthe Brasserie
and Bar** [46]
398 Hayes Street
San Francisco, CA 94102
T   415 551 1590
F   415 255 2385
E   talk@absinthe.com
W www.absinthe.com

Addison Endpapers [169]
6397 Telegraph Avenue
Oakland, CA 94609
T   510 601 8112

**African American Historical
& Cultural Society** [94]
Fort Mason Center, Building C
San Francisco, CA 94123
T   415 441 0460
W www.fortmason.org/museums/
index.html#african

Alabaster [171]
597 Hayes Street
San Francisco, CA 94102
T   415 558 0482
F   415 558 0587
E   alabaster@mindspring.com
W www.alabastersf.com

**Alameda Point Antiques
Market** [104]
Alameda Point Naval Station
Corner of Main Street and West
Atlantic Avenue
Alameda, CA 94501
T   510 522 7500
F   510 864 9198
E   info@antiquesbythebay.net
W www.antiquesbythebay.net

Alla Prima [69]
1420 Grant Avenue
San Francisco, CA 94133
T   415 397 4077
539 Hayes Street
San Francisco, CA 94102
T   415 864 8180

Amoeba Music [54]
1855 Haight Street
San Francisco, CA 94117
T   415 831 1200
W www.amoebamusic.com

Amphora Wine Merchant [46]
384A Hayes Street
San Francisco, CA 94102
T   415 863 1104
F   415 863 0926
W www.amphorawine.com

Anú [24]
43 Sixth Street
San Francisco, CA 94102
T   415 543 3505
W www.anu-bar.com

April in Paris [84]
55 Clement Street
San Francisco, CA 94118
T   415 750 9910
    415 775 1775 (Suzanne George)
F   415 750 9995
E   bea@aprilinparis.us
W www.aprilinparis.us

**The Archbishop's
Mansion** [120]
1000 Fulton Street
San Francisco, CA 94117
T   415 563 7872
F   415 885 3193
W www.jdvhospitality.com

Aria [69]
1522 Grant Avenue
San Francisco, CA 94133
T   415 433 0219

The Arion Press [83]
1802 Hays Street, The Presidio
San Francisco, CA 94129
T   415 561 2542
F   415 561 2545
E   arionpress@arionpress.com
W www.arionpress.com

Arléquin [46]
384B Hayes Street
San Francisco, CA 94102
T   415 626 1211
F   415 863 0926
E   arlequin@madwills.com

Arrow Bar [24]
10 Sixth Street
San Francisco, CA 94103
T   415 255 7920

Asian Art Museum [46]
200 Larkin Street
San Francisco, CA 94102
T   415 581 3500
F   415 581 4700
E   pr@asianart.org
W www.asianart.org

**Bacchus Wine and
Sake Bar** [90]
1954 Hyde Street
San Francisco, CA 94109
T   415 928 2633

The Bar [80]
340 Presidio Avenue
San Francisco, CA 94115
T   415 409 4901

Baraka [141]
288 Connecticut Street
San Francisco, CA 94107
T   415 255 0370
W www.barakasf.net

Bauerware [53]
3886 17th Street
San Francisco, CA 94114
T   415 864 3886
F   415 864 3889
E   inquiries@bauerware.com
W www.bauerware.com

Bay Bread Boulangerie [77]
2325 Pine Street
San Francisco, CA 94115
T 415 440 0356

Beach Chalet [57]
1000 Great Highway
Golden Gate Park
San Francisco, CA 94121
T 415 386 8439
F 415 386 4125
W www.beachchalet.com

Bell'Occhio [50]
8 Brady Street
San Francisco, CA 94103
T 415 864 4048
E postale@bellocchio.com
W www.bellocchio.com

Berkeley Rose Garden [103]
Euclid Avenue and Bayview Place
Berkeley, CA
T 510 644 6530
W www.ci.berkeley.ca.us/cool
   things/parks/rosegarden.html

Bette's Oceanview Diner [100]
1807 Fourth Street
Berkeley, CA 94710
T 510 644 3230
E bettesdiner@worldpantry.com
W www.worldpantry.com/bettes/
   home.html

B44 [19]
44 Belden Place
San Francisco, CA 94104
T 415 986 6287
F 415 986 6291
W www.b44.citysearch.com

Bimbo's 365 Club [155]
1025 Columbus Avenue
San Francisco, CA 94133
T 415 474 0365
E info@bimbos365club.com
W www.bimbos365club.com

Bi-Rite Market [38]
3639 18th Street
San Francisco, CA 94110
T 415 241 9760
F 415 241 9870
E info@biritemarket.com
W www.biritemarket.com

Bissap Baobab [151]
2323 Mission Street
San Francisco, CA 94110
T 415 826 9287
Little Baobab
3388 19th Street
San Francisco, CA 94110
T 415 643 3558
E bissap@keurbaobab.net
W www.keurbaobab.net

Blue Plate [137]
3218 Mission Street
San Francisco, CA 94110
T 415 282 6777

Boulange de Polk [90]
2310 Polk Street
San Francisco, CA 94109
T 415 345 1107

Braunstein/Quay Gallery [24]
430 Clementina Street
San Francisco, CA 94103
T 415 278 9850
F 415 278 9841
E bquayg@pacbell.net
W www.bquayartgallery.com

Bruno's [39]
2389 Mission Street
San Francisco, CA 94110
T 415 648 7701
W www.brunoslive.com

Burger Joint [35]
807 Valencia Street
San Francisco, CA 94110
T 415 824 3494
F 415 285 5267
W www.burgerjointsf.
   citysearch.com

The Butler and the Chef [27]
155A South Park
San Francisco, CA 94107
T 415 896 2075
W www.thebutlerandthechef.com

C. Bobby's Owl Tree [20]
601 Post Street
San Francisco, CA 94109
T 415 776 9344

Café Bastille [19]
22 Belden Place
San Francisco, CA 94104
T 415 986 5673
F 415 986 1013
E olivier@cafebastille.com
W www.cafebastille.com

Café Claude [19]
7 Claude Lane
San Francisco, CA 94108
T 415 392 3515
F 415 392 2226
E info@cafeclaude.com
W www.cafeclaude.com

Café de Stijl [62]
1 Union Street
San Francisco, CA 94111
T 415 291 0808

Café Fanny [146]
1603 San Pablo Avenue
Berkeley, CA 94702
T 510 526 7664
W www.cafefanny.com

Café Flore [146]
2298 Market Street
San Francisco, CA 94114
T 415 621 8579
W www.cafeflore.com

Café Jacqueline [70]
1454 Grant Avenue
San Francisco, CA 94133
T 415 981 5565

Café Niebaum-Coppola [65]
916 Kearny Street
San Francisco, CA 94133
T 415 291 1700
E sanfrancisco@cafecoppola.com
W www.cafecoppola.com

Caffe Centro [27]
102 South Park
San Francisco, CA 94107
T 415 882 1500
W caffecentro.com

Caffe 817 [104]
817 Washington Street
Oakland, CA 94607
T 510 271 7965

Caffe Trieste [149]
601 Vallejo Street
San Francisco, CA 94133
T 415 392 6739
F 415 550 1239
E info@caffetrieste.com
W www.caffetrieste.com

**California Palace of the
Legion of Honor** [84]
Lincoln Park
34th Avenue & Clement Street
San Francisco, CA 94121
T 415 863 3330
W www.thinker.org

Cartoon Art Museum [23]
665 Mission Street
San Francisco, CA 94105
T 415 227 8666
E office@cartoonart.org
W www.cartoonart.org

The Castro Theatre [54]
429 Castro Street
San Francisco, CA 94114
T 415 621 6120
E castroweb@aol.com
W www.thecastrotheatre.com

Catharine Clark Gallery [16]
49 Geary Street, 2nd Floor
San Francisco, CA 94108
T 415 399 1439
F 415 399 0675
E morphos@cclarkgallery.com
W www.cclarkgallery.com

César [153]
1515 Shattuck Avenue
Berkeley, CA 94709
T 510 883 0222
E info@barcesar.com
W www.barcesar.com

Cheese Board Collective [103]
1504 Shattuck Avenue
Berkeley, CA 94709
T 510 549 3183
W www.cheeseboardcollective.coop

Chez Nous [77]
1911 Fillmore Street
San Francisco, CA 94115
T 415 441 8044

**Chez Panisse Restaurant
and Café** [138]
1517 Shattuck Avenue
Berkeley, CA 94709
T 510 548 5525 (restaurant)
   510 548 5049 (café)
W www.chezpanisse.com

Chez Papa Bistrot [41]
1401 18th Street
San Francisco, CA 94110
T 415 824 8210
W www.chezpapasf.com

Chez Spencer [130]
82 14th Street
San Francisco, CA 94103
T 415 864 2191
F 415 864 2199
W www.chezspencer.com

**Chinese Historical Society of
America** [71]
965 Clay Street
San Francisco, CA 94108
T 415 391 1188
F 415 391 1150
E info@chsa.org
W www.chsa.org

Church of Christ Scientist [103]
2619 Dwight Way
Berkeley, CA 94704

Cielo [77]
2225 Fillmore Street
San Francisco, CA 94115
T 415 776 0641

Citizen Cake [135]
399 Grove Street
San Francisco, CA 94102
T 415 861 2228
F 415 861 0565
W www.citizencake.com

Citron [131]
5484 College Avenue
Oakland, CA 94618
T 510 653 5484
F 510 653 9915
W www.citron-acote.com

**City Lights Bookseller &
Publisher** [168]
261 Columbus Avenue
San Francisco, CA 94133
T 415 362 8193
F 415 362 4921
E staff@citylights.com
W www.citylights.com

Claremont Resort & Spa [126]
41 Tunnel Road
Berkeley, CA 94705
T 510 843 3000
W www.claremontresort.com

Clift [110]
495 Geary Street
San Francisco, CA 94102
T 415 775 4700
F 415 441 4621
E clift@ianschragerhotels.com
W www.clifthotel.com

Coit Tower [62]
1 Telegraph Hill
San Francisco, CA 94133
T   415 362 0808
W www.coittower.org

Columbarium [84]
1 Loraine Court
San Francisco, CA 94118
T   415 771 0717

Columbine Design [69]
1541 Grant Avenue
San Francisco, CA 94133
T   415 434 3016
E   info@columbinedesign.com
W www.columbinedesign.com

Conor Fennessy [69]
801 Columbus Avenue
San Francisco, CA 94133
T   415 673 0277
E   inquire@conorfennessy.com
W www.conorfennessy.com

**Creative Growth
Art Center** [104]
355 24th Street
Oakland, CA 94612
T   510 836 2340
F   510 836 0769
E   info@creativegrowth.org
W www.creativegrowth.org

Crissy Field [94]
Shoreline of the Presidio
Between the Palace of Fine Arts
and Fort Point
T   415 561 7690
W www.crissyfield.org

Da Flora [140]
701 Columbus Avenue
San Francisco, CA 94133
T   415 981 4664

Dalva [35]
3121 16th Street
San Francisco, CA 94103
T   415 252 7740

Dark Garden [166]
321 Linden Street
San Francisco, CA 94102
T   415 431 7684
F   415 431 7699
W www.darkgarden.com

De Vera [171]
29 Maiden Lane
San Francisco, CA 94102
T   415 788 0828
F   415 788 0831
E   info@deveraobjects.com
W www.deveraobjects.com

Delfina [132]
3621 18th Street
San Francisco, CA 94110
T   415 552 4055

Den [36]
849 Valencia Street
San Francisco, CA 94110
T   415 282 6646
F   415 282 6642

E   info@densf.com
W www.densf.com

Desiree [84]
39 Mesa Street, Suite 107
T   415 561 2336
F   415 561 2337
W www.sffilmcenter.com

Destino [50]
1815 Market Street
San Francisco, CA 94103
T   415 552 4451
F   415 552 4438
W www.destinosf.com

Diana Slavin [162]
3 Claude Lane
San Francisco, CA 94108
T   415 677 9939
F   415 677 9641
E   info@dianaslavin.com
W www.dianaslavin.com

Diesel [19]
101 Post Street
San Francisco, CA 94108
T   415 982 7077
F   415 982 7070
W www.diesel.com

Doña Tomas [104]
5004 Telegraph Avenue
Oakland, CA 94609
T   510 450 0522
W www.donatomas.com

Edinburgh Castle [21]
950 Geary Street
San Francisco, CA 94109
T   415 885 4074

871 Fine Arts [16]
49 Geary Street, 4th floor
San Francisco, CA 94108
T   415 543 5155

826 Valencia [36]
826 Valencia Street
San Francisco, CA 94110
T   415 642 5905
W www.826valencia.org

El Rio [39]
3158 Mission Street
San Francisco, CA 94110
T   415 282 3325
W www.elriosf.com

Emmy's Spaghetti Shack [41]
18 Virginia Avenue
San Francisco, CA 94110
T   415 206 2086

Erica Tanov [100]
1827 Fourth Street
Berkeley, CA 94710
T   510 849 3331
W www.ericatanov.com

Exploratorium [94]
Palace of Fine Arts
3601 Lyon Street
San Francisco, CA 94123
T   415 561 0360
W www.exploratorium.edu

Farley's [148]
1315 18th Street
San Francisco, CA 94107
T   415 648 1545

Farmers' Market [164]
Ferry Building
Market Street at Embarcadero
San Francisco, CA 94111
W www.ferryplazafarmers
     market.com

Ferry Building [164]
Market Street at Embarcadero
San Francisco, CA 94111
E   info@ferrybuilding
     marketplace.com
W www.ferrybuilding
     marketplace.com

Fetish [80]
344 Presidio Avenue
San Francisco, CA 94115
T   415 409 7429

Fleur de Lys [136]
777 Sutter Street
San Francisco, CA 94109
T   415 673 7779
F   415 673 4619
W www.fleurdelyssf.com

Flight 001 [49]
525 Hayes Street
San Francisco, CA 94102
T   415 487 1001
E   info@flight001.com
W www.flight001.com

Foreign Cinema [135]
2534 Mission Street
San Francisco, CA 94110
T   415 648 7600
F   415 648 7669
W www.foreigncinema.com

Fraenkel Gallery [16]
49 Geary Street, 4th floor
San Francisco, CA 94108
T   415 981 2661
F   415 981 4014
E   mail@fraenkelgallery.com
W www.fraenkelgallery.com

Friend [175]
401 Hayes Street
San Francisco, CA 94102
T   415 552 1717
W www.friend-sf.com

**Galeria de la Raza
and Studio 24** [41]
2857 24th Street
San Francisco, CA 94110
T   415 826 8009
F   415 826 6235
E   info@galeriadelaraza.org
W www.galeriadelaraza.org

**Garden Court & Pied Piper
Bar** [23]
The Palace Hotel
2 New Montgomery Street
San Francisco, CA 94105
Garden Court:
T   415 546 5010

F   415 537 6299
W www.gardencourt-
     restaurant.com
Pied Piper Bar:
T   415 546 5089

The Gardener [100]
1836 Fourth Street
Berkeley, CA 94710
T   510 548 4545
F   510 548 6357
E   store@thegardener.com
W www.thegardener.com

George [174]
2411 California Street
San Francisco, CA 94115
T   415 441 0564
1844 Fourth Street
Berkeley, CA 94710
T   510 644 1033
W www.georgesf.com

Gimme Shoes [162]
50 Grant Avenue
San Francisco, CA 94108
T   415 434 9242
2358 Fillmore Street
San Francisco, CA 94115
T   415 441 3040
416 Hayes Street
San Francisco, CA 94102
T   415 864 0691
E   info@gimmeshoes.com
W www.gimmeshoes.com

Globe [62]
290 Pacific Avenue
San Francisco, CA 94111
T   415 391 4132

Grace Cathedral [90]
1100 California Street
San Francisco, CA 94108
T   415 749 6300
W www.gracecathedral.org

Greens Restaurant [94]
Fort Mason, Building A
San Francisco, CA 94123
T   415 771 6222
F   415 771 3472
W www.greensrest.citysearch.com

The Grocery Store [80]
3625 Sacramento Street
San Francisco, CA 94118
T   415 928 3615

Haas-Lilienthal House [79]
2007 Franklin Street
San Francisco, CA 94109
T   415 441 3000
W www.sfheritage.org/house.html

Haines Gallery [16]
49 Geary Street, Suite 540
San Francisco, CA 94108
T   415 397 8114
F   415 397 8115
E   info@hainesgallery.com
W www.hainesgallery.com

Harputs [77]
1527 Fillmore Street
San Francisco, CA 94115

T 415 923 9300
E harputs@aol.com
W www.harputs.com

Hayes Street Grill [46]
320 Hayes Street
San Francisco, CA 94102
T 415 863 5545
E patty@hayesstreetgrill.com
W www.hayesstreetgrill.com

Hayes and Vine [46]
377 Hayes Street
San Francisco, CA 94102
T 415 626 5301

Hear Music [100]
1809B Fourth Street
Berkeley, CA 94710
T 510 204 9595
W www.hearmusic.com

Heather [77]
2408 Fillmore Street
San Francisco, CA 94115
T 415 409 4410

**Henri Baumann
Les Parfums** [168]
210 Post Street, Suite 511
San Francisco, CA 94108
T 415 982 1500
W www.henribaumann.com

Home [50]
2100 Market Street
San Francisco, CA 94114
T 415 503 0333
W www.home-sf.com

Hosfelt Gallery [24]
430 Clementina Street
San Francisco, CA 94103
T 415 495 5454
F 415 495 5455
E info@hosfeltgallery.com
W www.hosfeltgallery.com

Hotel Biron [50]
45 Rose Street
San Francisco, CA 94102
T 415 703 0403
E patrick@hotelbiron.com
W www.hotelbiron.com

Hotel Bohème [124]
444 Columbus Avenue
San Francisco, CA 94133
T 415 433 9111
F 415 362 6292
E info@hotelboheme.com
W www.hotelboheme.com

Hotel Griffon [116]
155 Steuart Street
San Francisco, CA 94105
T 415 495 2100
F 415 495 3522
E reservations@hotelgriffon.com
W www.hotelgriffon.com

Hotel Majestic [112]
1500 Sutter Street
San Francisco, CA 94109
T 415 441 1100
F 415 673 7331

E info@thehotelmajestic.com
W www.thehotelmajestic.com

Hotel Rex [122]
562 Sutter Street
San Francisco, CA 94102
T 415 433 4434
F 415 433 3695
W www.jdvhospitality.com

hrm [36]
924 Valencia Street
San Francisco, CA 94110
T 415 642 0841
E bob@hrmclothing.com
W www.hrmclothing.com

Huf [163]
808 Sutter Street
San Francisco, CA 94109
T 415 614 9414
E info@hufsf.com
W www.hufsf.com

Huntington Hotel [114]
1075 California Street
San Francisco, CA 94108
T 415 474 5400
F 415 474 6227
W www.huntingtonhotel.com

Imperial Tea Court [149]
1411 Powell Street
San Francisco, CA 94133
T 415 788 6080
E customerservice@
imperialtea.com
W www.imperialtea.com

International Orange [78]
2044 Fillmore Street, 2nd floor
San Francisco, CA 94115
T 415 563 5000
F 415 563 5500
E info@internationalorange.com
W www.internationalorange.com

Intersection for the Arts [35]
446 Valencia Street
San Francisco, CA 94103
T 415 626 2787
F 415 626 1636
W www.theintersection.org

Isa [93]
3324 Steiner Street
San Francisco, CA 94123
T 415 567 9588
F 415 409 1879

Jack Hanley Gallery [35]
389 & 395 Valencia Street
San Francisco, CA 94103
T 415 522 1623
F 415 522 1631
E jackhanley@aol.com
W www.jackhanley.com

Jade Bar [46]
650 Gough Street
San Francisco, CA 94102
T 415 869 1900
W www.jadebar.com

Jai Yun [143]
923 Pacific Avenue

San Francisco, CA 94133
T 415 981 7438
E jaiyun@menuscan.com
W www.jaiyun.menuscan.com

James Nicholson Gallery [16]
49 Geary Street, 4th floor
San Francisco, CA 94108
T 415 397 0100
F 415 397 0155
E info@nicholsongallery.com
W www.nicholsongallery.com

Japonesque Gallery [173]
824 Montgomery Street
San Francisco, CA 94133
T 415 391 8860

Jeremys [27]
2 South Park
San Francisco, CA 94107
T 415 882 4929
F 415 896 6738
E mail@jeremys.com
W www.jeremys.com

Juicy News [77]
2453 Fillmore Street
San Francisco, CA 94115
T 415 441 3051

Just for You [41]
732 22nd Street
San Francisco, CA 94107
T 415 647 3033
W www.justforyoucafe.com

Kabuto A & S [84]
5121 Geary Boulevard
San Francisco, CA 94118
T 415 752 5652
W www.kabutosushi.com

Kate Spade [19]
227 Grant Avenue
San Francisco, CA 94108
T 415 216 0880
F 415 216 0878
W www.katespade.com

Kayo Books [20]
814 Post Street
San Francisco, CA 94109
T 415 749 0554
E kayo@kayobooks.com
W www.kayobooks.com

**Kermit Lynch Wine
Merchant** [165]
1605 San Pablo Avenue
Berkeley, CA 94702
T 510 524 1524

Kiehl's [78]
2360 Fillmore Street
San Francisco, CA 94115
T 415 359 9260
W www.kiehls.com

Kyo-Ya [136]
The Palace Hotel
2 New Montgomery Street
San Francisco, CA 94105
T 415 546 5090
F 415 537 6299

E palacerestaurants.00373@
luxurycollection.com
W www.kyo-ya-restaurant.com

La Taqueria [143]
2889 Mission Street
San Francisco, CA 94110
T 415 285 7117

Laku [36]
1069 Valencia Street
San Francisco, CA 94110
T 415 695 1462

Laszlo [154]
2526 Mission Street
San Francisco, CA 94110
T 415 401 0810

Le Colonial [20]
20 Cosmo Place
San Francisco, CA 94109
T 415 931 3600
F 415 931 2933
E info@lecolonialsf.com
W www.lecolonialsf.com

Li Po [156]
916 Grant Avenue
San Francisco, CA 94108
T 415 982 0072

Ligne Roset [27]
162 King Street
San Francisco, CA 94107
T 415 777 1030
F 415 777 1345
W www.ligne-roset-usa.com

Liguria Bakery [66]
1700 Stockton Street
San Francisco, CA 94133
T 415 421 3786

Limn [27]
290 Townsend Street
San Francisco, CA 94107
T 415 543 5466
F 415 543 5971
W www.limn.com

Limón [38]
3316 17th Street
San Francisco, CA 94110
T 41 252 0918
F 415 252 0000
E limonrestaurant@yahoo.com
W www.limon-sf.com

Lion Pub [80]
2062 Divisadero Street
San Francisco, CA 94115
T 415 567 6565

Lit [24]
101 Sixth Street
San Francisco, CA 94103
T 415 278 0940

Lone Palm [156]
3394 22nd Street
San Francisco, CA 94110
T 415 648 0109
F 415 560 6619
W www.lonepalm.citysearch.com

Luggage Store [24]
1007 Market Street
San Francisco, CA 94103
T   255 5971
F   863 5509
W www.luggagestoregallery.org

Luna Park [137]
694 Valencia Street
San Francisco, CA 94110
T   415 553 8584
F   415 553 8660
E   hello@lunaparksf.com
W www.lunaparksf.com

**Lyle Tuttle Tattoo
Art Museum** [69]
841 Columbus Avenue
San Francisco, CA 94133
T   415 775 4991
W www.lyletuttle.com

**MAC (Modern Appealing
Clothing)** [161]
387 Grove Street
Sam Francisco, CA 94102
T   415 837 0615

Marc Jacobs [16]
125 Maiden Lane
San Francisco, CA 94108
T   415 362 6500
W www.marcjacobs.com

March [80]
3075 Sacramento Street
San Francisco, CA 94115
T   415 931 7433
W www.marchsf.com

**Mario's Bohemian
Cigar Store** [66]
566 Columbus Avenue
San Francisco, CA 94133
T   415 3620536
W www.mariosbohemian
     cigarstore.com

Mecca [50]
2029 Market Street
San Francisco, CA 94114
T   415 621 7000
F   415 621 7094
E   sfmecca@yahoo.com
W www.sfmecca.com

Medium Rare Records [53]
2310 Market Street
San Francisco, CA 94114
T   415 255 7273
F   415 255 7274

Merenda [93]
1809 Union Street
San Francisco, CA 94123
T   415 346 7373

Metier [160]
355 Sutter Street
San Francisco, CA 94108
T   989 5395
W www.metiersf.com

Mexican Museum [94]
Fort Mason Center, Building D
San Francisco, CA 94123

T   415 202 9700
F   415 441 7683
E   info@mexicanmuseum.org
W www.mexicanmuseum.org

Mission Dolores [38]
3321 16th Street
San Francisco, CA 94114
T   415 621 8203
F   415 621 2294
E   doloressf@aol.com
W www.missiondolores.
     citysearch.com

Moe's Books [103]
2476 Telegraph Avenue
Berkeley, CA 94704
T   510 849 2087
E   moe@moesbooks.com
W www.moesbooks.com

Mondo Gelato [103]
2106 Shattuck Avenue
Berkeley, CA 94704
T   510 883 1568
E   berkeley@mondogelato.com
W www.mondogelato.com

Murik [16]
73 Geary Street
San Francisco, CA 94108
T   415 867 5769
W www.murikstore.com

Museo ItaloAmericano [94]
Fort Mason Center, Building C
San Francisco, CA 94123
T   415 673 2200
F   415 673 2292
E   museo@firstworld.net
W www.museoitaloamericano.org

**Museum of Craft &
Folk Art** [94]
Fort Mason Center, Building A
San Francisco, CA 94123
T   415 775 0991
F   415 775 1861
W www.mocfa.org

Nancy Boy [52]
2319 Market Street
San Francisco, CA 94114
T   415 626 5021
F   415 626 5055
E   contact@nancyboy.com
W www.nancyboy.com

Nest [172]
2300 Fillmore Street
San Francisco, CA 94115
T   415 292 6199
2340 Polk Street
San Francisco, CA 94109
T   415 292 6198

Nickie's BBQ [54]
460 Haight Street
San Francisco, CA 94117
T   415 621 6508
W www.nickies.com

Noc Noc [54]
557 Haight Street
San Francisco, CA 94117
T   415 861 5811

Noon [50]
1637 Market Street
San Francisco, CA 94103
T   415 567 1555

O Chamé [100]
1830 Fourth Street
Berkeley, CA 94710
T   510 841 8783
W www.ochamerestaurant.com

**Oliveto Restaurant
and Café** [139]
5655 College Avenue
Oakland, CA 94618
T   510 547 5356
E   info@oliveto.com
W www.oliveto.com

111 Minna Gallery [154]
111 Minna Street
San Francisco, CA 94105
T   415 974 1719
E   minna@111minnagallery.com
W www.111minnagallery.com

Original Joe's [21]
144 Taylor Street
San Francisco, CA 94102
T   415 775 4877

Original Levi's Store [19]
300 Post Street
San Francisco, 94108
T   415 501 0100
W www.levis.com

Palace of Fine Arts [94]
3301 Lyon Street
San Francisco, CA 94123
T   415 563 6504
F   415 567 4062
E   info@palaceoffinearts.org
W www.palaceoffinearts.org

**Paramount Theatre
of the Arts** [104]
2025 Broadway
Oakland, CA 94612
T   510 465 6400
F   510 893 5098
W www.paramounttheatre.com

Paolo [77]
1971 Sutter Street
San Francisco, CA 94115
T   415 885 5701
F   415 885 5702
524 Hayes Street
San Francisco, CA 94102
T   415 552 4580
F   415 552 4582
E   info@paoloshoes.com
W www.paoloshoes.com

Pauline's Pizza Pie [35]
260 Valencia Street
San Francisco, CA 94103
T   415 552 2050

Paxton Gate [170]
824 Valencia Street
San Francisco, CA 94110
T   415 824 1872
W www.paxton-gate.com

Persian Aub Zam Zam [157]
1633 Haight Street
San Francisco, CA 94117
T   415 861 2545

Phoenix Hotel [118]
601 Eddy Street
San Francisco, CA 94109
T   415 776 1380
F   415 885 3109
W www.thephoenixhotel.com

Piperade [140]
1015 Battery Street
San Francisco, CA 94111
T   415 391 2555
W www.piperade.com

Pizzetta 211 [134]
211 23rd Street
San Francisco, CA 94121
T   415 379 9880
W www.pizzetta211.com

Plouf [19]
40 Belden Place
San Francisco, CA 94104
T   415 986 6491
F   415 986 6492
W www.plouf.citysearch.com

The Presidio [83]
Entrances on Presidio Boulevard,
West Pacific Avenue, Lyon Street
and Marine Drive
T   415 561 5300
W www.presidio.gov

Prize [90]
1415 Green Street
San Francisco, CA 94109
T   415 771 7215

Propeller [49]
555 Hayes Street
San Francisco, CA 94102
T   415 701 7767
E   info@propeller-sf.com
W www.propeller-sf.com

Recchiuti Confections [165]
One Ferry Building, no. 30
San Francisco, CA 94111
T   415 834 9494
W www.recchiuticonfections.com

Red's Java House [27]
The Embarcadero, Pier 30
San Francisco, CA 94101
T   415 777 5626

Redwood Room [152]
Clift Hotel
495 Geary Street
San Francisco, CA 94102
T   415 929 2372
W www.clifthotel.com

rnm [54]
598 Haight Street
San Francisco, CA 94117
T   415 551 7900
F   415 551 7901
E   info@rnm.com
W www.rnmrestaurant.com

Rolo [52]
2351 Market Street
San Francisco, CA 94114
T 415 431 4545
E contact@rolo.com
W www.rolo.com

Rosamunde Sausage Grill [54]
545 Haight Street
San Francisco, CA 94117
T 415 437 6851

Rosewood [153]
732 Broadway
San Francisco, CA 94133
T 415 951 4886

Samovar Tea Lounge [52]
498 Sanchez Street
San Francisco, CA 94114
T 415 626 4700
E info@samovartea.com
W www.samovartea.com

**San Francisco Art
Institute** [93]
800 Chestnut Street
San Francisco, CA 94133
T 415 771 7021
E sfaiinfo@sfai.edu
W www.sanfranciscoart.edu

Satin Moon Fabrics [80]
32 Clement Street
San Francisco, CA 94118
T 415 668 1623

SBC Park [27]
King Street
San Francisco, CA
T 415 972 2400 (tours)
W www.sfgiants.com

Scuderia West [35]
69 Duboce Avenue
San Francisco, CA 94103
T 415 621 7223
F 415 621 2589
E info@scuderiawest.com
W www.scuderia.com

SF Camerawork [28]
1246 Folsom Street
San Francisco, CA 94103
T 415 863 1001
F 415 863 1015
E sfcamera@sfcamerawork.org
W www.sfcamerawork.org

SFMOMA [22]
151 3rd Street
San Francisco, CA 94103
T 415 357 4000
F 415 357 4037
W www.sfmoma.org

Six [24]
60 Sixth Street
San Francisco, CA 94103
T 415 863 1221
E info@clubsix1.com
W www.clubsix1.com

Slanted Door [142]
The Ferry Building
San Francisco, CA 94111
T 415 861 8032
F 415 861 8329
E eat@slanteddoor.com
W www.slanteddoor.com

Slow Club [41]
2501 Mariposa Street
San Francisco, CA 94110
T 415 241 9390
W www.slowclub.com

Smith Williams [163]
1827 Union Street
San Francisco, CA 94123
T 415 346 4280
F 414 346 8904
E smith@smithwilliams
   stores.com
W www.smithwilliamsstores.com

**Specs' Twelve Adler Museum
Café** [66]
12 Adler Place
San Francisco, CA 94133
T 415 421 4112

South Park Café [24]
108 South Park
San Francisco, CA 94107
T 415 495 7275

The Stud [28]
399 9th Street
San Francisco, CA 94103
T 415 252 7883
E stud@studsf.com
W www.studsf.com

Sue Fisher King [80]
3067 Sacramento Street
San Francisco, CA 94115
T 415 922 7276
W www.suefisherking.com

SumBody [93]
2167 Union Street
San Francisco, CA 94123
T 415 775 6343
E orders@sumbody.com
W www.sumbody.com

Suppenküche [49]
525 Laguna Street
San Francisco, CA 94102
T 415 252 9289
F 415 252 8661
E sable@suppenkuche.com
W www.suppenkuche.com

Susan [80]
3685 Sacramento Street
San Francisco, CA 94118
T 415 922 3685

Sushi Groove [90]
1916 Hyde Street
San Francisco, CA 94109
T 415 440 1905

Sushi Groove South [28]
1516 Folsom Street
San Francisco, CA 94103
T 415 503 1950

Swallowtail [90]
2217 Polk Street
San Francisco, CA 94109
T 415 567 1555
F 415 567 1503
E info@swallowtailhome.com
W www.swallowtailhome.com

Swan Oyster Depot [142]
1517 Polk Street
San Francisco, CA 94109
T 415 673 1101

Tacubaya [100]
1788 Fourth Street
Berkeley, CA 94710
T 510 525 5160

Tadich Grill [62]
240 California Street
San Francisco, CA 94111
T 415 391 1849

Tail of the Yak [104]
2632 Ashby Avenue
Berkeley, CA 94705
T 510 841 9891

Tallula [53]
4230 18th Street
San Francisco, CA 94114
T 415 437 6722
F 415 437 6723
W www.tallulasf.com

Tartine Bakery [147]
600 Guerrero Street
San Francisco, CA 94110
T 415 487 2600
F 415 487 2605
E info@tartinebakery.com
W www.tartinebakery.com

Thomas E. Cara Ltd [65]
517 Pacific Avenue
San Francisco, CA 94133
T 415 781 0383

Tien Hua Temple [71]
125 Waverly Place
San Francisco, CA 94108

Timo's [36]
842 Valencia Street
San Francisco, CA 94110
T 415 647 0558
F 415 647 0573
W www.timos.com

Tonga Room [151]
The Fairmont Hotel
950 Mason Street
San Francisco, CA 94108
T 415 772 5283
W www.tongaroom.com

Toronado [54]
547 Haight Street
San Francisco, CA 94117
T 415 863 2276
F 415 621 0322
E info@toronado.com
W www.toronado.com

Tosca Café [155]
242 Columbus Avenue
San Francisco, CA 94133
T 415 986 9651

Transamerica Pyramid [65]
600 Montgomery Street
San Francisco, CA 94111
W www.tapyramid.com

Tru [65]
750 Kearny Street
San Francisco, CA 94108
T 415 399 9700
W www.truspa.com

True Sake [49]
560 Hayes Street
San Francisco, CA 94102
T 415 355 9555
F 415 987 0053
E info@truesake.com
W www.truesake.com

Tu Lan [24]
8 Sixth Street
San Francisco, CA 94103
T 415 626 0927

Universal Café [134]
2814 19th Street
San Francisco, CA 94110
T 415 821 4608

Varnish [24]
77 Natoma Street
San Francisco, CA 94105
T 415 222 6131
F 415 222 6137
W www.varnishfineart.com

**Verdigris Clay Studio and
Gallery** [175]
The Cannery, 2nd floor
2801 Leavenworth Street
San Francisco, CA 94133
T 415 440 2898
E thegallery@verdigrisgallery.com
W www.verdigrisgallery.com

Vesuvio [66]
255 Columbus Avenue
San Francisco, CA 94133
T 415 362 3370
E vesuvio@vesuvio.com
W www.vesuvio.com

Vicolo Pizzeria [46]
201 Ivy Alley
San Francisco, CA 94102
T 415 863 2382
W www.hayesstreetgrill.com

Vik's Chaat Corner [100]
724 Allston Way
Berkeley, CA 94710
T 510 644 4412
W www.vikdistributors.com

Vivande Porta Via [79]
2125 Fillmore Street
San Francisco, CA 94115
T 415 346 4430
F 415 346 2877
E info@vivande.com
W www.vivande.com

Voda [19]
56 Belden Place
San Francisco, CA 94104
T 415 677 9242

Walzwerk [28]
381 South Van Ness Avenue
San Francisco, CA 94103
T 415 551 7181
F 415 551 7182
W www.walzwerk.com

Wave Organ [94]
Marina Green
Yacht Road
San Francisco, CA
W www.exploratorium.edu/
    visit/wave_organ.html

**William K. Stout Architectural
Books** [65]
804 Montgomery Street
San Francisco, CA 94133
T 415 391 6757
F 415 989 2341
E libri@stoutbooks.com
W www.stoutbooks.com

Wingard [93]
2127 Union Street
San Francisco, CA 94123
T 415 345 1999
F 415 345 9909
E info@wingardinc.com
W www.wingardhome.com

Woodward's Garden [28]
1700 Mission Street
San Francisco, CA 94103
T 415 621 7122
W www.woodwardsgarden.com

Workshop [93]
2254 Union Street
San Francisco, CA 94123
T 415 561 9551

Xanadu Gallery [16]
140 Maiden Lane
San Francisco, CA 94108
T 415 392 9999
F 415 984 5856
E info@xanadugallery.us
W www.xanadugallery.us

XOX Truffles [66]
754 Columbus Avenue
San Francisco, CA 94133
T 415 421 4814
F 415 530 2099
W www.xoxtruffles.com

X21 Modern [36]
890 Valencia Street
San Francisco, CA 94110
T 415 647 4211
F 415 695 0797
E info@x21modern.com
W www.x21modern.com

Yank Sing [22]
One Rincon Center
101 Spear Street

San Francisco, CA 94105
T 415 957 9300
W www.yanksing.com

**Yerba Buena Center
for the Arts** [23]
701 Mission Street
San Francisco, CA 94103
T 415 978 2787
W www.yerbabuenaarts.org

**Yuet Lee Seafood
Restaurant** [70]
1300 Stockton Street
San Francisco, CA 94133
T 415 982 6020

Zazu & Violet's Hats [167]
1790 Shattuck Avenue
Berkeley, CA 94709
T 510 845 1409

Zeitgeist [35]
199 Valencia Street
San Francisco, CA 94103
T 415 255 7505
E zeitgeistsf@earthlink.net
W www.zeitgeist.citysearch.com

Zinc Details [100]
1842 Fourth Street
Berkeley, CA 94710
T 510 540 8296
F 510 540 8289
E info@zincdetails.com
W www.zincdetails.com

Zonal [49]
568 Hayes Street
San Francisco, CA 94102
T 415 255 9307

Zuni Café [133]
1658 Market Street
San Francisco, CA 94102
T 415 552 2522

CALISTOGA [178]
*From San Francisco, go north over
the Golden Gate Bridge, follow
Highway 101 to Santa Rosa, then
take the River Road/Mark West
Springs Exit. Turn right onto Mark
West Springs and continue for ten
miles before turning left onto
Petrified Forest Road. At Highway
128, turn right, and follow for one
mile. At the sign for Calistoga, turn
left onto Lincoln Avenue and follow
it a few blocks to the end. Indian
Springs is on the right.*

Indian Springs
1712 Lincoln Avenue
Calistoga, CA 94515
T 707 942 4913
F 707 942 4919
E info@indiansprings
    calistoga.com
W www.indiansprings
    calistoga.com
Bungalows from $250

Clos Pegase
1060 Dunaweal Lane
Calistoga, CA 94515
T 707 942 4981
F 707 942 4993
E info@clospegase.com
W www.clospegase.com

PESCADERO [180]
*Head south on Highway 1. The last
major town you will pass through is
Half Moon Bay, about 26 miles from
Costanoa. 10.5 miles before you
reach Costanoa you will see signs
for the historic town of Pescadero.
Do not turn, continue south on
Highway 1. After passing a large
grove of Eucalyptus trees on your
left, the entrance road to Costanoa
(Rossi Road) is signposted and is
the only left hand turn on the
highway.*

Costanoa Coastal Lodge & Camp
2001 Rossi Road
Pescadero, CA 94060
T 650 879 1100
F 650 879 2275
E costanoa@costanoa.com
W www.costanoa.com
Rooms from $150

Duarte's Tavern
202 Stage Road
Pescadero, CA
T 650 879 0464
F 650 879 1460
W www.duartestavern.com

Bonny Doon Winery
2 Pine Flat Road
Santa Cruz, CA 95060
T 831 425 4518
F 831 425 3528
W www.bonnydoonwinery.com

HEALDSBURG [182]
*From San Francisco, go north over
the Golden Gate Bridge and follow
Highway 101 for 67 miles. Take the
Central Healdsburg exit. Go straight
on Healdsburg Avenue until you
reach the town plaza
(approximately 1.25 miles). Turn left
onto Matheson Street and the Hotel
entrance will be on your right.*

Hotel Healdsburg
25 Matheson Street
Healdsburg, CA 95448
T 707 431 2800
F 707 431 0414
E frontoffice@
    hotelhealdsburg.com
W www.hotelhealdsburg.com
Rooms from $250

Dry Creek Kitchen
317 Healdsburg Avenue
Healdsburg, CA 95448
T 707 431 0330
F 707 431 8990
W www.charliepalmer.com

Jimtown
6706 State Highway 128
Healdsburg, CA 95448
T 707 433 1212
F 707 433 1252
E jimtown@jimtown.com
W www.jimtown.com

INVERNESS [184]
*After crossing the Golden Gate
Bridge, head north for 8.5 miles,
and take the exit for San Anselmo,
and at the last minute, for Sir
Francis Drake Boulevard. Take this
road and head west for
approximately 21 miles, at which
point you will have come to coastal
Highway 1. Turn right and head
north for exactly two miles, where
you will see a sign for Inverness.
Turn left. When you do you will be
back on Sir Francis Drake
Boulevard, the tail end of which is
the main road on the peninsula.
Drive four miles, which will put you
in the village of Inverness. Go
another block and a half beyond the
only gas station, and turn left on
Argyle. Come up a steep hill a few
hundred yards. Manka's is an old
hunting lodge which is on your
right.*

Manka's Inverness Lodge
P.O. Box 1110, Inverness
T 415 669 1034
E mankas@best.com
W www.mankas.com
Rooms from $190

Hog Island Oysters
PO Box 829
Marshall, CA 94940
T 415 663 9218
F 415 663 9246
E hogislnd@svn.net
W www.hogislandoysters.com